Baptist Principles

To my good friend
Bill Martin —
With respect, esteem, with
best personal wishes — but
especially with gratitude that we
have shared some of this Baptist
journey together.

George H. Tooze
December 2012

Endowed by
TOM WATSON BROWN
and
THE WATSON-BROWN FOUNDATION, INC.

BAPTIST PRINCIPLES

With Practical Applications and Questions for Discussion

George H. Tooze

MERCER UNIVERSITY PRESS
MACON, GEORGIA

The James N. Griffith Series in Baptist Studies

This series on Baptist life and thought explores and investigates Baptist history, offers analyses of Baptist theologies, provides studies in hymnody, and examines the role of Baptists in societies and cultures around the world. The series also includes classics of Baptist literature, letters, diaries, and other writings.

—Walter B. Shurden, Series Editor

MUP/ P464

1400 Coleman Avenue
Macon, Georgia 31207

First Edition

Books published by Mercer University Press are printed on acid-free paper that meets the requirements of the American National Standard for Information Sciences—Permanence of Paper for Printed Library Materials.

Mercer University Press is a member of Green Press Initiative (greenpressinitiative.org), a nonprofit organization working to help publishers and printers increase their use of recycled paper and decrease their use of fiber derived from endangered forests. This book is printed on recycled paper.

ISBN 978-0-88146-438-2

Cataloging-in-Publication Data is available from the Library of Congress

This volume is lovingly dedicated to

My students from the Church Leadership Institute
The American Baptist Churches of Indianapolis, and
The American Baptist Churches of Indiana, Kentucky

My students from Christian Theological Seminary
Indianapolis, Indiana

My colleagues at, and the members of
First Baptist Church, Gardner, Massachusetts
First Baptist Church, Beverly, Massachusetts,
First Baptist Church, Malden, Massachusetts
First Baptist Church of Indianapolis, Indiana

Your intellectual curiosity, your deep faith, your interest in being Baptist, your probing questions, your fruitful discussion, your superb presentations—all over many years—is the genesis that gave birth to this volume.

To God Be the Glory!

Contents

Preface / ix

Acknowledgments / xv

1. Baptist Roots: A History / 1

2. Soul Freedom / 16

3. Autonomy of the Local Church / 44

4. Believer's Baptism / 59

5. Biblical Authority / 83

6. The Lord's Supper / 116

7. The Priesthood of the Individual Believer / 129

8. Regenerate Church Membership / 153

9.The Separation of Church and State / 166

Concluding Thoughts / 191

Preface

I am a Baptist by heritage. My mother was raised in the Park Street Baptist Church, Framingham, Massachusetts where she became a Sunday School teacher and a "Guild Girl" (The World Wide Guild.)[1] She died as a member of the Brewster Baptist Church in Brewster, Massachusetts. My father was raised Roman Catholic, but began to attend the Baptist church with my mother when they were married in 1931. I remember him being baptized and joining the church when I was a young child, probably about six years old (which would have been 1945).

I am a Baptist by birth. When I was born in May of 1939, my parents had just purchased a house in Randolph, Massachusetts, and so I was added to the Cradle Roll of the First Baptist Church of Randolph. It was there that I went to Sunday school and worship (every Sunday—no exceptions); it was there I became active in the youth group (I obtained my driver's license, my first car, and started in the youth group all about the same time). Sunday school teachers and youth leaders, as well as my pastors played formative roles in my life, and I remember them as God's saints, for that's what they were to me. When I felt that I had a call to ministry, they affirmed that call, and they credentialed me, giving me, with a vote from the church, what then was a License to Preach the Gospel.

I am a Baptist by choice. I have studied the Scriptures and thought much about Baptist polity. I believe that we Baptists in form and practice model what we see in the Bible, especially when we speak of the Baptist Principles. In other words I am not a Baptist today simply because of inertia.

I also find that I am a Baptist by temperament. Soul freedom defines my personality for I have an inquiring, questioning mind, and I always want to know "what?" and "how?" and "why?" Certainly I have strong convictions, but I am aware that we live in a pluralistic society (and hopefully Church). Thus, dialogue around our differences is to me an essential part of the meaning of community. It is how we do this, with

---

[1] The World Wide Guild originated around the turn of the twentieth century out of the leadership of the Mission Societies of the Northern Baptist Convention as a program for girls and young women. It was intended as a mentoring program to pass on to the next generation values of faith and mission.

respect, trust, encouragement, and civility, that defines how each of lives out our faith and convictions. I dislike it when someone tries to impose an idea or an action on me; I want to take time to think about it, come to my own conclusion, and/or have the right to differ with another. As I see it, these personal characteristics are all Baptist to the core.

It may be that I have been called upon more than some to be thoughtful about these matters of Baptist Principles. I had served First Baptist Church of Gardner, Massachusetts, as a student minister (1963–4), First Baptist Church of Beverly, Massachusetts, as an associate minister (1964–77), and First Baptist Church of Malden, Massachusetts, as a senior minister (1977–83). I came to First Baptist Church of Indianapolis, Indiana, in the fall of 1983.

In 1983, the Indianapolis church was just emerging from ten years of conflict. A twenty-three-year pastoral ministry had been followed by a three-year ministry, which had been followed by the rejection of a recommended candidate by the church body. The minister before me had been asked to leave after twenty-five months, and as he moved on, half of the congregation decided it was time to move on to other congregations as well. One of the issues that had been contentious was the church's relationship to American Baptist Churches, USA. Many of the members had joined the church in previous years without a personal, historic, denominational relationship, and they saw no need for such an institutional relationship to continue. This also spilled over into conflicts around curriculum choices, expenditure of mission dollars, and relationships with regional and national judicatories. Countering this new group was a strong corpus with historic American Baptist heritage and alliance. To them, it was important that the church maintain its alliance with the American Baptist Churches. It was this latter group that had stayed on when the equally large group had left. As I came on board, the search committee, and later the leadership, let me know that remaining affiliated with The American Baptist Churches was of extreme importance, and that I was to do everything in my power to enable the strongest possible relationship. This meant that I was to be active in the life of the denomination, serve on committees and boards at every level when asked, to attend association, state, and national denominational meetings, and to promote the denominational mission offerings. Looking back, I take great pride in my involvement and in what continues to be a strong and meaningful part of my life, as I have stayed active in denominational leadership.

Not long into my pastorate in Indianapolis I began to realize that many of the members of the church who had remained after the split had not come from Baptist backgrounds. I found that this was increasingly true of the new members who were joining us.

I decided early on to preach a series on Baptist Principles that received, for the most part, enthusiastic response (one older member did shake her head and inform me that she saw neither purpose nor value in them). Over twenty years of ministry, those sermons were updated and reworked—in 1997 we celebrated our 175th anniversary, and I was again asked by the Anniversary Committee to preach on the Principles. Interestingly, I found that over those years my own thinking and understanding had continued to grow, and I was somewhat surprised by the differences between the earlier and later sermons. Of course, having an additional fourteen years of pastoral experience helped immeasurably.

In the early part of this new century, I was asked to teach the Baptist Polity Course for the Church Leadership Institute program of the American Baptist Churches of Indianapolis and the American Baptist Churches of Indiana/Kentucky. It was at this point that I really had to do some deeper and much-broader thinking. Having half a dozen sermons in your file on Baptist Principles is hardly sufficient to fill twenty-four hours of teaching time on the subject. Even my files containing Baptist themes that I had accumulated over the years, while helpful, were certainly not enough to carry the ball.

Furthermore, in the winter of 2009 I was asked to teach the Baptist Polity class at Christian Theological Seminary (Disciples of Christ) in Indianapolis. That brought a new challenge, for the needs of the seminarian classroom were quite different than a classroom for lay ministry students. In addition, the teaching time was extended to a daunting thirty-nine hours.

Both of these opportunities challenged me to thoughtfully and purposefully pull together all of my material into "teachable" content.

This book, as it has emerged, is intended to serve three segments of our Baptist life. It is first of all for individuals, pastors and laity, who want to do serious thinking about Baptist Principles, working through the tensions and applying their evolving conclusions to their own personal life and ministry. It is secondly for students, those theologically trained and those not trained except for their life within the local Baptist church, and especially for those who sense a further and deeper commitment to that involvement. It is thirdly for pastors and church leadership who want to dialogue together towards common ministry goals and who seek a deeper understanding of what differentiates us as Baptists. The book hopes to declare and define the tensions that are inherent in any Baptist congregation because the potential for differences of faith and interpretation are enormous. Each of the Baptist Principles can lead us in any number of directions.

Throughout this volume you will find a number of scenarios that were intended to encourage my students to think about the practical, everyday church and life implications of Baptist Polity and Principles. These scenarios began to come to me one day as I looked for something with which to introduce each seminary class, to produce a discussion that would be timely and to the point, yet have some depth to it. I also wanted the Baptist principle discussion to be informed out of my forty years of pastoral ministry, helping me to share and apply my experiences with those just entering ministry. Putting this book together has been a wonderfully creative process—one that keeps coming to me as I write and think at deeper levels in each of the areas. Originally I needed thirteen scenarios—one for each class in the semester—and now there are forty-five in this volume, covering seven subjects, and three for general topics. Several people who visited my class to make presentations, or who participated in the opening discussion, were kind enough to ask for copies of the scenarios, and they have begun to bring back stories of the discussions generated by their using them in personal settings. The comments have been most gratifying, and I do confess that as I listened to their very kind remarks, I began to think that I had further reason to pull all of this together into a book.

A number of you who read this book and take it seriously may think that portions of it are outrageous, that some of the scenarios are ill conceived, and that some of the probing questions I ask about the scenarios are "off the wall." My students and parishioners will be glad to hear that for they are not immune to those same thoughts; you and they join many of those who have sat in the pews and listened to my sermons these many years who have also entertained similar responses. When they come to me bothered, expressing their anxieties, their troubled thoughts, and grasping for what seems to be an illusive truth, I tell them that I am in complete agreement with them; yes, I am intentionally pushing their buttons, and some of this is over the edge. But then I go on to say that I'm simply trying to make them (you) think. I want them (you) to be able to be articulate in the face of questions that are being asked in the Church and in the world. I want them (you) to be able to articulate answers from their own heart and mind that are strong, viable, and convincing both to themselves and others. My experience, most generally and graciously, has been that, when it is all over, they thank me, because in the end I have not tried to change their minds. That would not be the Baptist way. But what I hope they do have is a stronger foundation upon which to stand, and upon which to build the ministries in the churches they will go on to attend and serve. They can speak with conviction from a sure foundation.

Being a Baptist is a thoughtful process and indeed can be a lot of effort and work. Sometimes our thinking goes against the grain and is difficult for others to comprehend or understand it. For example, try telling someone that you do not believe in public prayer in our school systems. Confess that you do not believe that there should be an American flag in the church sanctuary. Declare that you do not believe that baptism by immersion should be an absolute requirement for membership in a Baptist church. Articulate that, in your view, theological and Biblical openness demands acceptance of welcoming and affirming churches within denominational life. As you run those subjects around in your thinking, you will begin to understand why it is that not everyone thinks that the openness of Baptist Principles, (or at least this particular version of that openness,) is something they want to own or even think about. This is true of many Baptists, some even in the circles in which we all are involved.

In the end, if you read the entire book, if you answer the questions following the scenarios thoughtfully, if you get in some strong dialogue with other believers (with some who agree with you and with some who do not), then you may understand my intentions. It is here that we come to the most important part; you *can make up your own mind* about these issues. I suspect you will also realize you are just beginning, that a constantly shifting landscape calls for more study and dialogue. This, of course, is the meat and potatoes of Baptist life, and that is what is so precious about being Baptist (at least in my mind). It is both our conviction and our practice.

I am proud of my Baptist Heritage, and grateful that I have been enabled to make a contribution in this way. I hope it strengthens the lives and the ministries of others.

I am extremely pleased that I am able to reach into my years of pastoral experience and bring illustrations to the text as I look at the polity and principle challenges I have faced within the life of the church. There have been many challenges that have shaped, even changed my thought; they are not, I am sure, unique to me, and I believe that you will find some resonance in them. To share these ideas and experiences has been a wonderful extension of my own pastoral ministry of these past forty years.

In your reading and dialogue, and in your journey, I wish for you all of God's blessings. Take great pride in your Baptist roots, for we believe that the Spirit of God has been in our development, and certainly in the living out of our personal faith.

George H. Tooze, Jr.
Indianapolis, Indiana

Acknowledgments

I would like to thank the following for carefully reading this manuscript, returning it with thoughtful questions and suggestions. Their work has greatly enhanced its effectiveness.

The Reverend Doctor Nick Carter, Newton Centre, Massachusetts;
The Very Reverend Robert Giannini, Indianapolis, Indiana
The Reverend Doctor Sumner Grant, New York, New York;
The Reverend Doctor Dennis Johnson, Charleston, West Virginia;
Mrs. Constance Taylor Tooze, Indianapolis, Indiana.
Dr. G. Andrew Tooze, Winston-Salem, North Carolina

1

Baptist Roots: A History

Baptist Roots

Because of our contentious ways, certain Baptists have said with a smile that we can trace our heritage back to the early days of the Old Testament when Jacob supposedly said to Esau, "You go your way and I'll go mine."

There are some who would say that we emerged from the disciples of John the Baptist. The Landmarkists express a theory of secessionism, with a thread of Believer's Baptism traceable through history in what they define as the "only true Church;" this thread or line begins with the baptism of Jesus by John the Baptist, which they would argue was by immersion. With this, the immersion principle (and Baptism) has been preserved through a series of dissident churches and movements that have separated themselves from the mainstream of Church history. Baptist Churches, therefore, and specifically Landmark Baptist Churches, see themselves as the one true New Testament Church because of their continuous line of practicing Believer's Baptism by immersion. Unfortunately scholarship does not support this idea, and perhaps the nail in the coffin was the discovery by W.H. Whitsitt, in his perusal of original English manuscripts from the seventeenth century, that the early Baptists practiced sprinkling as their form of baptism[1] in the early years 1609 to 1641.[2]

---

[1] James H. Slatton, *W.H. Whitsitt: The Man and the Controversy* (Macon GA: Mercer University Press, 2009).

[2] His eventual documentation and publication of this fact was so contentious that he was relieved of his presidential position at Southern Seminary in Louisville, Kentucky. One detractor stated very clearly that if a prominent Baptist through "freedom of expression" should come to conclusions "destructive of Baptist principles," then "the one arriving at such a conclusion should not be permitted to remain among us." In ancient times this was akin to "killing the messenger."

The Power of the Time Line

Looking back over two millennia of history, we have a tendency to generalize. We see the beginning of themes and events; then, we see a middle section where these themes and events are being played out. Finally we see an ending, how everything turned out and how things were resolved. Our tendency, however, as we look back through time is to view earlier events through the prism of the ending. In other words, we know how the story is going to end, so we minimize the passion of the years, the anxiety of the participants, and the human emotion and drama. We fail to note the terrible tensions that resolve, with tremendous cost, into peaceful progress.

Several years ago I picked up the Abraham Lincoln Civil War biography by Doris Kerns Goodwin, *Team of Rivals*.[3] Upon his election, Lincoln pulled together a cabinet of some of the best minds of the era, even though a number of them had been significant and contentious personal political rivals against him and against each other. Several of them, including Secretary of State William Seward,[4] were clear in their thinking that Lincoln was mismatched for the presidency, and they were not hesitant to share those opinions. Lincoln believed that the country needed the best he could bring to the table, and that the rivalry and distrust of his cabinet could be overcome and a cohesive team could rise from the disparity. I was surprised how well Goodwin captured those moments in history when everything hung in the balance, when there was no guarantee that the Union would prevail, when the leadership factions were destructive and could have imploded. We are not conditioned to look for such beginning and middle events. We remember how Seward, now personally transformed from his relationship with Lincoln, wept with powerful grief when the president was killed. We know that the Union was victorious and the country remained intact, so the times that threatened gravely never materialized and thus seem unimportant.

---

[3] Doris Kearns Goodwin, *Team of Rivals* (New York: Simon and Schuster, 2006).

[4] William Seward's claim to fame as Secretary of State was the purchase of the Alaska Territory for the United States, which then became known as "Seward's Folly."

So it is with Baptist History. We have our Baptist Principles so we know what came out of history, how in fact the story ended. What we miss, however, are the people and events that brought us to this place. What happened over sixteen centuries that created fertile ground for emergent Baptists? What were the sixteenth- and seventeenth-century events that changed our history Who were the people that seized the challenge and brought Baptists into being? It is my intent to go back to the beginning and discover some of the junctures that were critical to the forward movement, including the tensions and the animosities, the tiny steps over many centuries that brought us to where we are today. My intention is to illustrate the beginning and the middle so that we understand how we arrived at the ending.

The Historic Church

In truth Baptists emerged out of sixteen hundred years of an established Church, as we protested, or stood against, certain beliefs and practices. We were identified as "protesters" or "protest-ants." As early as the fifteenth century, and perhaps even the fourteenth century, the central themes were beginning to emerge. By this I mean to say that if you take any one of the Baptist Principles, there are numerous interpretations as to its meaning and practice. We might say, for example, that "Soul Freedom" is a Baptist Principle, but how we interpret it, and how we see it being implemented is often disparate. We will look at some of these differences in the individual chapters on the Principles.

However, before we identify these emergent themes and how we wove them together, let's take a look at those sixteen hundred years of history beginning with the early Church and the New Testament, which it birthed, particularly those elements that created dissonance and rebellion.

In the Gospels, Jesus did not leave a blueprint for the Church. He spoke to the disciples of mission and responsibility, but there was nothing about its becoming a structure, an institution, a denomination. Jesus did tell Peter that he was a rock, and upon that rock—which we believe was not Peter but his faith statement—he would build his Church. Peter was told that he would be given the keys of the kingdom, that whatever he bound on earth would be bound in heaven, that whatever he loosed on earth would be loosed in heaven. Peter was also promised that the gates of hell would not be able to prevail against the Church (Mt 5:13-20, NRSV).

Notwithstanding the dialogue with Peter, in another instance Jesus denied James and John seats in this kingdom at his right and left hand (Mt 20:20-23).[5] Talking of leadership, Jesus spoke of the least being the greatest and the greatest being the least, a flimsy structure at best for an organization (Lk 9:48).[6] In the end, Jesus simply told the disciples to go out on to the byways and into the villages and proclaim the gospel modeled after his own announcement in early Mark: "The time is fulfilled, and the kingdom of God has come near; repent, and believe in the good news" (Mk 1:15).

In the Book of Acts we see an emerging church structure. It is increasingly obvious that the imminent return of Jesus Christ is not going to take place as the early Church expected it to. Early Church leaders had believed the word of the angel as spoken in Acts 1:11; that they would see Jesus return from heaven even as they had seen him ascend into heaven. But it had not happened, and now the Church is growing and spreading; discipline and organization are desperately needed. Deacons are set aside so that the apostles can stay with the important proclamation. It would seem that James, the brother of Jesus, and Peter, the disciple, shared leadership. Peter is obviously a key leader, but in the Council of Jerusalem in Acts 15 it is James before whom Paul appears. This Council of Jerusalem wrestled with a structure to handle some of the issues growth demanded, and from this moment we begin to see an emergent organization.

Paul speaks of leaders being appointed, indicating an increasingly larger structure. In First Timothy, chapter three Paul mentions the requirements for bishops and deacons,[7] and he presents very clear lists of

---

[5] The mother of James and John asked this of Jesus, but he declared them unable to drink the same cup as he. Jesus then said that it was not his to give, but the prerogative belonged to "my Father."

[6] While the disciples were speaking amongst themselves, discussing which of them was the greatest, Jesus picked up a child and said that "the least among all of you is the greatest."

[7] The Greek is *episkopon* and *diakonous*, translated in NRSV as "bishop" and "deacon," and in the American Bible Society's Good News as "a church leader" and "church helpers."

what those qualifications would involve. These are not educational requirements, nor is there an emphasis on training or prior service and experience. Rather they are personal characteristics like honesty, sobriety, reputation, respect, and capability of teaching and of leading a loving family environment.

Historically we know that the house worship centered around the celebration of the Agape meal. Members would open their homes to others to break bread and share the cup as Jesus had commanded them to do. They would share their memories of Jesus, tell their personal stories, and gain courage to face the hostile world that increasingly was persecuting them. We can see some of the edges of this persecution in the accusations of Celsus,[8] who said that the Christians were cannibalistic because they ate the body and drank the blood of their fallen leader. We are strongly struck by the fact that this persecuted Church became a strong Church, for a persecuted Church draws as witnessing believers only the most transformed and committed, those willing to pay whatever price was necessary to belong to Jesus Christ.

In his recent book,[9] Harvard theologian Harvey Cox writes about the early Church, and he makes a wonderful case for its diversity: The Church of the first three centuries lacked the universality and unanimity we often attribute to it. Instead, as it expanded, it picked up individualistic qualities from different geographic areas and cultures, and it moved in practice and doctrinal understanding in numerous directions. There was not, as we would like to believe, a uniformity; there were the Christians, and the Judiazers, and what came to be the Gnostics, Ebionites, Montanists, Arians, Pelagians, Novatians, Donatists to mention a few. The common thread was that the Holy Spirit was at work leading and directing—empowering—and that differences of interpretation and understanding were not a factor. In fact, if you look at the epistles of Paul, he spoke mostly to practices in the Church—sexual immorality, treatment of people—but not of doctrinal purity.

---

[8] Celsus wrote in the days of early Christian persecution. His book, *The True Word*, was an anti-Christian polemic. While no copies of this book have survived, one of the church fathers, Origin, wrote a book *Contra Celsum*, which gave a Christian apologetic, arguing against each point made by Celsus.

[9] Harvey Cox, *The Future of Faith* (New York: HarperOne, 2009.)

Everything changed within the Church in 313 when the emperor Constantine made the Church the official Faith of his empire. He hoped that Christianity would become a unifying, cohesive factor. To accomplish this unification it was very important, with increasing pressure, that the Church resolve any internal differences it might have. Lack of conflict and the appearance of solidarity trumped a passion for spiritual and redemptive transformation.

The passionate Biblical faith of a persecuted but faithful at all costs Church was diluted to complacency by the sheer weight of numbers and the insistent need for governance and control. Hoards were baptized whether they were sincere in their expression of faith or not. The meaning and practice of what it was to be a Christian became diluted to minimum expression, and the church became an "institution" as opposed to a mission or a ministry. Some historians would suggest that there was an equal dose of politics and religion in Constantine's move, and there is probably considerable truth in that observation. Building and organization seemed to become more important than a passionate faith lived out in witness and service.

Here creedalism was introduced. To bring uniformity of thought and expression Councils introduced carefully constructed doctrines which were considered absolute, and these were defined by the creeds. So it was that there was a shift from a Church culture where God's Holy Spirit was actively at work to a culture where faith became a subscription to a series of creedal affirmations.

In spite of the call for unity, these years were in many ways divisive, with the Church struggling to find its identity, defining it with theological dogma. One of the fiercest battles, for example, was against the Arian belief that Jesus Christ was not fully divine. The mantra of Arius was: "There was when the Son was not." In other words Jesus did not exist eternally in the Godhead with the Father and Holy Spirit, but rather he was created; created before the foundations of the earth, but nevertheless created. All through a significant portion of the fourth century the conflict between Athanasius (the bishop of Alexandria, Egypt) and Arius (A Christian presbyter from Alexandria, Egypt) played out. There were Councils where Athanasius prevailed and the divinity of Jesus Christ was proclaimed and where the Scriptural Canon was established. There was the emergence of the Bishop of Rome as the strongest and ultimately the dominant leader in the Church, though this was not without some historic challenges. At the end of this theological battle there was the great East – West divide between Rome and Constantinople, an ecclesiastical divide which exists to this day.

In the centuries that followed this structure governed by the Bishop of Rome became formalized and embedded, with the Church beginning to create enormous wealth for itself. The wealth came through dowries paid by the families of those who entered convents, through wealthy individuals leaving land and buildings to the Church, through the selling of indulgences[10] (special grace, obtained by monetary gift, sufficient to release a loved one from the flames of purgatory), and through the selling of Church Offices. This money was used for the building of massive church edifices and for the creation of gold and jeweled chalices and crosses to garnish magnificent altars. The art and jeweled objects in the Vatican Museum alone testify to this wealth, not to mention the land and properties held across the globe.

A supplement to the creation of wealth was the creation of power. The Church held within its hands the power of salvation. Only the priest could forgive sin, which meant at the time of death the difference between heaven and hell. Yet, there seemed to be a desire for even more, however, and during the Middle Ages there was significant tension as to who held temporal power, with kings and popes in contention with each other. A review of historical literature of this time will elicit many examples of this tension and how it played out. One example to illustrate a plethora of historical situations would be that in the early thirteenth century Giles of Rome wrote the book *On Ecclesiastical Power*. According to John Kilcullen, "Giles's book argues that the Pope's fullness of power extends to political matters, so that the Pope is the supreme ruler of the world, God's deputy on earth, who delegates power to governments and supervises their activities."[11]

---

[10] We are reminded of the great story of Johann Tetzel raising money for the building of St Peter's Basilica in Rome, going from village to village proclaiming the fiery images and intense suffering of burning in hell, ending with the chant, "Remember—as soon as the coin in the coffer rings—the soul from purgatory springs."

[11] John Kilcullen, "Medieval Political Policy, "*Stanford Encyclopedia of Philosophy*. The encyclopedia is maintained on Wikipedia by Stanford University.

With power and wealth came significant corruption. Pastoral offices were sold, and often held by families. Immorality was sometimes flagrant. Abuses permeated the system.[12] The point is simple: Corruption in the pre-Reformation Church was one of the stimulators to succession, that is churches leaving the established Church to form their own version based on truths as they were discovering them. These emerging Christians of different persuasion sought, through leaving and establishing a Church themselves, to purify their lives and the life of Church and Society.

Another issue for the medieval Church was the fact that Scripture was hardly available. First, there were few copies of it, for the labor to produce a copy of hand-written Scripture was excessive and limited to the monasteries. Every copy had to be hand copied, a word, a page at a time, from prior editions. Even if it had been available, however, the average person could not read, and all interpretation of Scripture had to be done by the priest through the services of the Church. In place of personal reading of Scripture, there were passion plays, roadside crosses with carvings on them, and murals in the churches that were used to visually teach the stories of Scripture for the members of a society who had no other way of learning them. Without access to the Scriptural text, its truth always came to individuals second-hand; individuals were dependent on someone else as a source of its information.

The fourteenth and fifteenth centuries brought dissenting voices that could not be ignored. Many of these voices came from within the Church, and foremost among them was Martin Luther. As Luther read

---

[12] From Wikibooks, the open-content textbooks collection: European History/The Crises of the Middle Ages: The Corruption of the Church. "The vast corruption in the church also led many to doubt and question its authority. The excess wealth of clergy and the frequency of clergymen having mistresses and illegitimate children was a major concern. The people also questioned the church's sale of indulgences, or receiving payment to forgive people of their sins; nepotism; simony, or the sale of church office; pluralism, or holding multiple church offices; and the extreme luxury of cathedrals." Even in the late twentieth century we have had more examples of this in both Protestant and Roman Catholic circles. We have seen dioceses bankrupted because of massive payouts to the victims of sexual abuse, and we have seen modern televangelists go to jail for misuse of funds, for indulging in lavish lifestyles, and for engaging prostitutes.

the Scriptures, especially the Epistle to the Romans, he began to see that grace was freely given and received, that salvation was but for the asking. There was no need for indulgences or pilgrimages, nor even for the Church as it then existed. God was ready at all times to embrace the sinner who approached God repentantly. Luther's original intent was to debate these matters within the Church, but the Church would broker no debate, and so the resulting schism was self-inflicted. Yet there was sufficient movement in other places that would have pushed forward what we have come to know as the Reformation.

Other Reformers

For the purpose of providing some concrete stepping stones, I want to review seven reformers or reform movements in addition to Luther who made significant challenges and changes that were encouragement as the Baptists pulled their principles together.

Ulrich Zwingli. Zwingli was in Zürich, Switzerland. He repudiated indulgences, transubstantiation (the physical presence of Jesus Christ in the Eucharist), and papal authority. He saw Communion as a memorial recalling the sacrificial work of Jesus Christ.[13]

Radical Reformers. These were Swiss Brethren, supporters of Zwingli. They opposed infant baptism, and "insisted that the New Testament knew only a believers' church."[14]

Balthazar Hubmaier. In 1524 Hubmaier wrote "Eighteen Dissertations Concerning the Entire Christian Life." Among these propositions he said—Faith alone makes us pious before God—all works of penance must be abandoned—the Mass is not a sacrifice but a memorial of the death of Christ—Images and pictures are of no value—(Jesus Christ) must be for us the only intercessor and mediator.[15]

The Anabaptists. "(They) affirmed the authority of the Bible, the priesthood of all believers, and the importance of faith alone for salvation. They rejected the claims of the Roman Catholic Church regarding councils, popes, and bishops. They suggested that the church is

---

[13] Bill J. Leonard, *Baptist Ways: A History* (Valley Forge PA: Judson Press, 2003) 19.

[14] Ibid.

[15] William L. Lumpkin, *Baptist Confessions of Faith* (Valley Forge PA: Judson Press, 1959) 20–21.

composed only of true believers, those who can testify to an experience of grace through repentance and faith. This profession is followed by baptism—a rite administered to believers only."[16]

The Anglican Church. The pope's refusal to allow Henry VIII a divorce from Catherine of Aragon forced separation, though there had been centuries of contest between monarch and pope over secular power.[17]

The Puritans. They were scattered in many ways, but their issues involved separating themselves from the Anglican Church to avoid its abuses and to put in place their own ideas about church governance. One of their strongest gifts was the idea of congregational authority.

The Separatists. A Separatist church in Gainsborough, England, was eventually to give birth to the Pilgrim group who left for the New World aboard the Mayflower, and in 1609 to a church in Amsterdam founded by John Smyth and Thomas Helwys. The foundational principles for the Amsterdam church included congregational polity and believer's baptism (though early on baptism was by sprinkling).[18]

The Transformative Invention

After centuries of Church development, with ferment growing within and without, history was ready for explosive change; it only needed something to ignite it.

That igniter was the invention of the printing press.

With the printing press, books could be quickly and uniformly printed, so that both the scholar and the common man had access to books, especially the Bible. Here they could turn its pages by themselves, could read its words, and, in an unfiltered process, could come to their own understanding of what the Bible taught and what it expected. Most importantly, they could compare what it said to current doctrine and practice.

Having brought us to this point I now want to tell you a story, a story that pulls together these last several hundred years of history, a story that shows the threads that were woven into Baptist fabric.

---

[16] Leonard, *Baptist Ways*, 20.

[17] Ibid., 21.

[18] Ibid., 23–25.

A Story About an Emergent Baptist

We note with interest that, unlike other churches, Baptists do not have a person or a point in time that defines us, like a Martin Luther, a John Calvin, or a John Wesley. We cannot point to a single time or event[19] when we became what we are; this is not our experience as Baptists. We were born in history, out of events, out of process, out of change, out of historical events, out of protest for certain principles which we felt to be of strong importance. Again, because of this we are a part of the protestant tradition where protestant means: "to stand for something," "to affirm a principle."

To tell the Baptist story and how Baptists came to be, let me tell you about one of our ancestors in the faith. His name was Johann, or John, and he lived in the northern part of the Swiss Alps, or in a part of Germany, or in the English countryside, or he could have been a dissenter moving to Holland in search of religious freedom to practice his faith according to his conscience.

John was a member of the established Church; it was, in fact, the only Church, and it had existed since the time of the apostles.

Because the Church had existed for centuries, it had traditions, and those traditions were a part of its authority. If one could not explain why things were the way they were, there was always a tradition upon which to fall back. "It has always been done this way. This is our history. We do not need a reason; we have a tradition."

John had been a part of the Church since birth when his parents brought him for baptism. The Church was his whole life. It had incredible power over his life and even his afterlife, for it alone determined his entrance into heaven or hell at the time of his death. If he was in accord with the Church and its faith, then he went to heaven; if he were not in accord, he would go to hell. If John was to be disobedient, the Church could withhold from him the sacraments, and without them he would be consigned to the torments of the dammed for all eternity. The

[19] Some might argue that the founding of the Amsterdam Congregation in 1609 by John Smyth and Thomas Helwys might approach such status. However, Smyth soon moved away from the congregation to seek membership with the Mennonites, and Helwys never assumed the foundational status of Luther, Calvin, or Wesley.

beauty of heaven was conditional upon obedience, not to the will of God, but to the power of the Church.

John, like most, was uneducated. He worked in the fields as a child, and his family depended completely on the labor he gave and the food he produced. His knowledge of the faith came entirely from the clergy, because only the clergy could read Scripture and thus interpret it. John saw the power of the Church even at work in the kingdom in which he lived. The Church controlled the political process so that not even the king dared to go against it. Many kings had their secular power challenged, and the authority of the Church was absolute over every portion of life.

Everything changed for John with the arrival of a neighbor who could read. Some years before, the invention of movable type and the ability to print a page inexpensively had changed the direction of history. The neighbor taught John to read, and the book they used as a lesson was a copy of the Bible. As John began to read, he began to think some strange thoughts. "My, my," he said to himself one day, "this doesn't seem to agree with what I heard in church on Sunday." As the months passed that became a common experience. He began to see on the pages of the Bible a slant, an affirmation, a system of belief, which was inconsistent in his mind with the teaching of the Church.

John began to say to himself as he read the Scripture: "Perhaps the clergy are wrong in the way they have been interpreting this; perhaps the Church is wrong in what it has taught us about some of these things; perhaps the Church should not have as much power and control over our lives as it does; perhaps the traditions have no basis in Scripture; perhaps there are different ways to interpret what we see before us."

One of the teachings that jumped out at him was the teaching about becoming a Christian. There seemed to be a process to faith in the Bible. First, there was the preaching of the Word, then there was the hearing of the Word, then there was belief and following the expression of that belief, there was baptism. John found a wonderful example of this in the story of the Ethiopian eunuch (Acts 8:26–40). Philip proclaimed or interpreted the gospel to the Ethiopian; the Ethiopian heard what Phillip was saying to him; he believed what Phillip was saying to him, and he asked for baptism. In the Bible, baptism was something that the believer experienced after this process had taken place. It could not be independent of the process, nor could it be at birth prior to the process, as it had happened to and for John. The principle began to emerge for John, and for those with whom he read the Bible, that the church should consist only of those whose lives have been changed through the work of the Holy Spirit, those who have professed their faith in Jesus Christ as Savior and Lord.

Because John believed that baptism is a result of faith, it had to be, in his view, a believer's experience, and only an adult could be a believer. Thus, John became what then was called an Anabaptist, which means to rebaptize. That is, they had been baptized as infants, but now they baptized each other again as believing adults, saying that their old baptism was no longer valid because it was not they who had made the choice but their parents who had made the choice for them.

As John joined together with others of like mind, these Anabaptist and other dissenters began to form their own vision of the Church, breaking with the authority of the Church and clergy over their lives.They sought their own interpretations of Scripture based on their life and experience and on their own scholarship. They affirmed that you became a Christian when you could affirm your own faith, and they said that baptism was only for believers.[20]

John and his fellow believers objected to statues in churches, saying that you should pray directly to God and not to an intermediator.[21] They also objected to the clerical dress, saying that it set the clergy apart and that this was not consistent with the belief of the priesthood of the individual believer, that is, that everyone has equal access to God. They objected to kneeling down at the Lord's Supper, saying that this implied adoration of the physical presence of Christ, which they did not feel was there. The bread and wine, they said, were but a memorial, a remembrance of Christ. They were not the actual body and blood of Jesus.

---

[20] It is interesting to note historically that immersion at the time was not an issue; the early Baptists rebaptized in many instances by sprinkling; immersion came in at a later date.

[21] I believe that this is the origin of our bowing our heads and closing our eyes when we pray. In those days when the Church was filled with statues, icons, carved screens, paintings, murals, if you were a Protestant, you simply ignored them by putting your head down and closing your eyes.

In John's story I have condensed several hundred years of history. These events moved slowly and there were inevitable detours and side excursions, but in John's life and story we discover the principles of who we are, as Baptists, and we see why the Principles emerged. It was in a sense the "fullness of time." The Church was emerging out of centuries of absolute control with its attendant frustrations. This history was intersecting with the rise of science and reason; Galileo had declared that the sun did not revolve around the earth as the Church had taught, and even though Galileo recanted that thought to save his life, the rising tide of enlightenment and reason showed the fallibility of the Church, exacerbating the reactions to its rigidity and moving society and culture into a New Age, which was to include Reformation.

For Baptists all these new ideas would come into focus in 1610. John Smyth and Thomas Helwys had already been expressing formative Baptist ideas and they would bring them together in the formation of a Baptist Church in Amsterdam. "All being equal, Smyth proposed that Helwys their social leader should baptize them, but he deferred to his spiritual leader. Smyth baptized himself, then baptized Helwys and the others. The mode was apparently trine affusion, pouring water three times in the name of the Father, the Son, and the Holy Spirit. The first Baptist church in the world was born with John Smyth's self-baptism."[22]

So it is that if you are a Baptist you will believe: (1) That the individual is competent to search the Scriptures and to make their own personal decision about its meaning and how that meaning should be lived out. Therefore, every person has the responsibility to search the Scripture and interpret it for themselves, and then to be in dialogue with others in the Church to test out their own thoughts and conclusions against the thoughts and conclusions of others. A part of this is the right of every person to worship in a manner dictated by their conscience. (2) That church membership is for believers only, a decision made as an adult, at the age of responsibility, and that believer's baptism follows the decision to become a believer; (3) That all of the decisions of the Church are in the hands of the congregation; there is no outside authority to that

---

[22] Jesse C. Fletcher, *The Southern Baptist Convention: A Sesquicentennial History* (Nashville: Broadman and Holman, 1994). I found this quote in Bill Leonard's *Baptist Ways* (Valley Forge PA: Judson Press, 2003) 25.

congregation; (4) That the Church is free from the interference of the civil authority, that the civil authority is free from the interference of the Church, and we give this the name Separation of Church and State; (5) That we are a Church where authority does not rest in tradition but solely in the Scripture; (6) That we are a Church where clergy and laity are the same before God, where all are priests able to stand before the throne of God seeking forgiveness of sins, seeking the healing of the Holy Spirit.

These are core Baptist Principles, and the rest of this book will look at a number of them in more detail, namely:

1. Soul Freedom
2. Autonomy of the Local Church
3. Believer's Baptism
4. Biblical Authority
5. Lord's Supper
6. Priesthood of the Individual Believer
7. Regenerate Church Membership
8. Separation of Church and State

As I interpret these Principles, I have added to the end of each chapter a number of scenarios as topics for discussion. These scenarios are an attempt to bring the Baptist Principles to life in the real world, and many of them have come out of my own pastoral experience. They are provocative and potentially divisive, for contention is built into our Baptist DNA. Soul Freedom encourages diversity of opinion, and this diversity can at times be significant and compelling. When passion meets passion it is only grace and love, not to mention the power of the Holy Spirit, that is able to keep us together.

2

Soul Freedom

One of our strongest foundational Baptist Principles is that of Soul Freedom; in fact I would go so far as to say it is the pre-eminent or essential Baptist Principle.[1] All other Principles are defined in relationship to it.

By Soul Freedom we mean the freedom we believe was given to us by God and is inherent in the creation of the human family. Accordingly, we believe that this is substantiated, that we find it implicit, throughout the pages of Scripture. In this chapter we will explore the images of Soul Freedom within biblical life.

One important definition of Soul Freedom is: "the historic affirmation of the inalienable right and responsibility of every person to deal with God without the imposition of creed, the interference of clergy, or the intervention of civil government."[2] Another thoughtful definition is: "the God-given freedom and ability of persons to know and respond to God's will. Baptists believe that God gives people competency—that is ability—to make choices."[3]

Thomas Helwys was an early Baptist Separatist and a 1609 founder of the first Baptist Church in Amsterdam, Holland. In 1612 he wrote *A Short Declaration of the Mystery of Iniquity*, and in that treatise he said: "Let the King judge, it not most equal that men should choose their religion themselves, seeing they only must stand themselves before the judgment

---

[1] In my original manuscript, the Baptist Principles were listed in alphabetical order. However, several who were asked to read the manuscript critically for me pointed out that Soul Freedom permeates my thinking on all of the Principles; it is, indeed, foundational. The decision was made to make it the first chapter so that the reader would be informed as they read subsequent chapters.

[2] Walter B. Shurden, *The Baptist Identity: Four Fragile Freedoms* (Macon GA: Smyth & Helwys Publishing, 1993) 23.

[3] "The Hostile Homilist," http://guybeaumont.blogspot.com/2009/03/Baptist-distinctive-soul-liberty.html.

seat of God to answer for themselves, when it shall be no excuse for them to say, We were commanded or compelled to be of this religion by the king or by them that had authority from him."[4]

With these broad definitions, let us look at some of the reasons as to why Baptists believe we find Soul Freedom in the Scripture. I will follow that with a section of illustrations from Scripture that give examples of Soul Freedom at work. Then I will move on to some applied principles and their more personal meaning to individuals of faith. Finally I will give a practical application in one particular area exploring in more detail our thinking.

The Argument for Soul Freedom in the Bible

The first signpost in identifying Soul Freedom[5] is the account in the Bible that tells us that we are created in the very image of God. The image of God, we believe, is imprinted on our soul. Yes, it is clouded and obscured at times by our human nature. If, however, we nurture our relationship with God, if we seek to discern the will of God, if we stop to listen to the voice of God, the image of God within can inform and shape our actions, our lives, and our commitment. The soul is competent to make decisions of faith and interpretation, as well as decisions on how, as people of faith, we will live our lives.

The second signpost indicating Soul Freedom is our belief that we as individual people of faith have direct access to God. With this we understand that we need no clergy, no minister or priest, no institution, no intermediary, to access God for us. We can do this because of our soul competency, and we can do this because of the redemptive work of Jesus Christ on the cross. Jesus opened the window of heaven to us, if you will. Or, to give a more Biblical image, at the time of his death on the cross, the curtain that divided the Holy Place and the Holy of Holies was split and opened (Lk 23:45), a statement acknowledging our direct access to God without inter-mediator. You will recognize, of course, that here we are speaking of the Baptist Principle of the Priesthood of the Individual Believer.

---

[4] Bill J. Leonard, *Baptist Ways: A History* (Valley Forge PA: Judson Press, 2003) 26.

[5] Another term used is "Soul Competency."

The third signpost suggesting Soul Freedom is the knowledge that we have the revelation of God to inform us. The primary place for this revelation is the Scripture, though we also believe that God is revealed to us other ways as well. These "other ways" might include prayer, the lives of fellow believers, and the natural world around us. In all of this God has opened God's self, God's universe, and God's ways that we might seek both to understand God and God's world, and with that to understand how we are to live faithfully within both. The Way is an open page before us, only to be deciphered, absorbed, and lived out.

The fourth signpost testifying to Soul Freedom is the freedom of choice that God gave to the man and the woman in the garden. God set them there and gave them the freedom to choose the direction of their lives. Though they abused it, the freedom of choice was, and continues to be, the awesome gift of God to the human family. So we have the freedom to read and interpret the Scriptures. We have the freedom not to be confined to a creed, not to be forced into a dogma. If you are living or worshipping in a place where you are told that you have to recite a creed, that you have to believe a particular dogma, then I can guarantee you that you are not in a Baptist Church, or at least what many Baptist purists would consider a "real" or an "authentic" Baptist Church.

Let me summarize and pull all four signifiers together in a whole: first there is the image of God in us put there by God as a part of the act of creation. Then there is our direct access to God. Next there is the revelation of God in many manifestations, but primarily Scripture, to inform us. Finally there is the freedom of choice to act. The constant thread that runs in and through it all is the personal privilege and responsibility that comes to each individual. It is our personal responsibility to follow these convictions and in so doing to seek the image of God, to study the revelation of God, and to make the right choices. This is our individualism! We are on our own! Yes! We are helped by others, and in dialogue with others, but ultimately it is our individual personal responsibility. "It is easy for us to yield our integrity and responsibility to some accepted authority: beloved pastor, honored teacher, influential book—even an edition of the Bible—respected parents or dynamic church. These all have their proper role of influence, but the final choice of belief and practice must be made in the secret of the soul's naked presence before God alone."[6]

So, when you begin to take part in the life of a Baptist church, you will idealistically find a group of people who study the Scriptures. Out of this study they will ask very difficult questions about this Bible and how to interpret it in formation of their faith, in seeking how to live out that faith both in the church and in the world. In search of God's truth and way, they will be in dialogue with each other, seeking to incorporate the discernment of others into their own thinking. They will impose no formal creeds or dogmas upon each other. They will agree to disagree with each other, sometimes passionately. But in the end, their love, respect, and trust for each other, their commitment to the Scripture, and their strong desire for ministry and mission will be sufficient to bind them together. Here, in the end, that tolerance of diversity in interpretation and understanding of God's will and word will be the foundation for community and common mission.

Freedom and Responsibility in the Bible

I have made the argument that the idea of personal freedom and the call for individual responsibility runs throughout the Biblical narrative. I now want to document that argument with some pertinent illustrations.

Freedom or individual choice is found in the call of the people of Israel to be the people of God. It would have begun with Abram's obedience of God's call to "the land that I will show you." (Gn 12:1) Abram had a choice in his response, as did his descendents. Set aside as the chosen people of God, bound to God by mutual covenant, they were given a privileged relationship with God that did not exist with any other nation. Through the temple and their rituals of worship, they had access to the presence of God. But they were always free to turn away in sin, to participate in the evil of the world, to reject God, or to worship other gods—which was often their choice of action. This is the story of the Old Testament, forty years in the wilderness, a new land, struggling between the temptations of Baal and the seductiveness of fertility worship, and the harsh requirements of God. In and through these eras of history, of rise

---

[6] C. Brownlow Hastings, *Introducing Southern Baptists: Their Faith and Their Life* (New York: Paulist Press, 1981) 24.

and fall and rise again, of faith and practice, of punishment and restoration, God sought to bring back the Israelites. Power and force could capture their attention. The Egyptians, the Assyrians, and the Romans could bring them to their knees as a warning sign from God, as a call to attention; but love and grace permeated the open arms of reconciliation.

The exercise of freedom or individual choice is found in the story of Daniel, forbidden by King Darius to worship any God other than Darius himself. Daniel had a difficult decision to make that could have cost him his life, but Daniel chose to defy the king, going "to his house, which had windows in its upper room open toward Jerusalem, and to get down on his knees three times a day to pray to his God and praise him, just as he had done previously" (Dn 6:10).[7]

This freedom and individual choice is found everywhere in the active ministry of Jesus. Jesus went out and issued an active invitation to "follow me," but there was no coercion other than the example of his life and the power of his words. He gave the invitation for repentance: "The kingdom God has come near; repent and believe in the good news (Mk 1:15)," but he made the response a personal decision on the part of the listener.

This freedom and individual choice is integral to the story of the work and the ministry of Jesus. Called to the cruel, redemptive cross to die, Jesus could have gone in another direction. The whole idea in Paul's writing about Jesus being the second Adam (Rom 5:12–19, 1 Cor 15:45) meant that Jesus could have said "no." Salvation demanded Jesus' perfect obedience; yet, had he not had the freedom to reject the cross, then his obedience would have been simply that of a robot. Jesus consciously and deliberately made the choice; without freedom, his obedience would have been empty.

Freedom and individual choice is found in the story of the apostles in Acts 5. The Pentecostal Spirit was at work in their lives, and their testimony was buttressed by "signs and wonders" to the point that the

---

[7] I am indebted to Charles W. Deweese and his article "Doing Freedom Baptist Style: Liberty of Conscience." I found it through a Google search. It is from a pamphlet, one of nine in the series, The Baptist Style for a New Century, jointly published by the Baptist History and Heritage Society and the William H. Whitsitt Baptist Heritage Society.

Jewish religious leaders, still not having received the message, responded in the only way they knew how—they arrested the apostles and put them into prison. Through a miracle of God's intervention, the apostles were released, whereupon they went back to the temple to begin preaching again, the very activity that had got them into trouble in the first place. Again they were called before the Sanhedrin and given "strict orders not to teach in this name," to which, with their awesome freedom of choice, they responded: "We must obey God rather than any human authority"[8] (Acts 5).

Freedom and individual choice is implicit in the words of Paul to the churches. He calls them to holiness, to cease those actions that separate them from God and from one another. The suggestion is always that of choice: They can continue in the ways of division, or they can change and draw near to God.

In all of the Scriptures, freedom is always tied to a profound sense of responsibility. While the people of God are free to choose, each choice has consequences and the people of God must accept the responsibility for the act of choice and the results that are forthcoming.

This is the lesson of Adam and Eve. By exercising their freedom and making a choice, they turned away from obedience to God. They did it decisively, yet, when called to accountability, Adam blamed Eve. "There I was in the garden," he said, "and she gave me the fruit to eat, and what could I do but eat it? It's all her fault." Poor, helpless Adam! With that, God turned to Eve, but she blamed the serpent. "The serpent beguiled me," she said; "I did not mean to do it, but he's a subtle one, he is. He twisted my arm. He tricked me. I did not mean to do it but I had no choice." God is not to be mocked by such foolishness. Holding Adam and Eve responsible, God cast them from the garden as punishment, and that meant death. The fruit of disobedience was death.

The people of God are held responsible for their actions. A case can be made that this is God punishing them, and an equal case could be made that God is correcting them; there may be elements of both, but in the end it felt the same to those receiving it. Jonah is held responsible for going in the opposite direction to that directed by God. Sent to Nineveh, he went another way, but he could not run far enough and was

[8] Ibid.

eventually brought back on course. There is freedom of choice, but there are also consequences. Ananias and Sapphira are held responsible for the act of lying to the apostles (Acts 5:1–11). Seeking the acclamation given to Barnabas for selling a piece of land and turning over the proceeds, Ananias and Sapphira also sold some land and turned over some of the proceeds, but they lied, saying they were turning over all of the proceeds as had Barnabas, when in fact they had held back some of the money. "You did not lie to us but to God!" said Peter, whereupon Ananias dropped dead, as later did Sapphira when she too was caught in the lie. Again, there is freedom of choice, but also consequences. David is held responsible for his adultery with Bathsheba (2 Sam 11, 12). David had climbed to the heights of national power and lofty favor as a child of God. There were, however, a number of instances when he descended to the absolute depths of irresponsibility; out of these choices he and his family paid a terrible price for his sin. And so it goes: absolute freedom to make choices, but always responsibility and accountability before God for the decision and the action.

Freedom is also tied to the love of God. Behind freedom there is unconditional love and grace and forgiveness. Adam and Eve were cast from the garden, but God continued to love them and to seek a way of bringing them back. God never forces obedience; it is a matter of choice. But God waits with open arms. That is the story of the prodigal son. It is the freedom of the son to leave and to do what he does. Yet when he returns home, his father waits and welcomes him with a loving heart.

Our individual freedom given by God as found in the Scriptures and coupled with responsibility has profound implications for our lives, for your life and for my life. It is the foundation for the way we experience and live out our faith.

Soul Freedom Applied Biblically

In this section we want to look at some of the ways in which the implications of Soul Freedom touch our personal and individual lives of faith.

First of all, there is the implication that we have the freedom to accept or to reject salvation. Salvation was accomplished on the cross. It is there, it is offered by God to all. It is undeserved; it is unearned. Nevertheless, it is available, ours for the asking. We can, we have to, make a choice. We can say "yes' or we can say "no." We can open our arms to it or we can reject it. Whatever, the consequences affect how we live here on earth, and they affect our eternal relationship with God.

Second, there is the implication that we have the freedom to live whatever kind of life we want to lead. Paul said that we could show evidence of the power of God working through our lives, or we could be slaves to the passions that are so much a part of our existence. We can control them or we can give them free reign to take us wherever they might. We can be bad, or we can be good. We can be sinners or we can be saints. We can hurt or we can heal. We can cast away or we can save. We can be hateful or we can love. We can be angry or we can seek to understand. We can separate ourselves or we can reconcile. We can be irresponsible or we can be responsible. In choice, there is always a tension of opposites. Paul was brutally honest about the tension: "I do not understand my own actions. For I do not do what I want, but I do the very thing I hate" (Rom 5:15–16).

Third, there is the implication that we have the freedom to worship God in a chosen way. In fact we even have the freedom not to worship God. We would say that such a choice is self- destructive; we would say that our souls desperately need to be fed by word and fellowship. We would say that we need to gather together as the body of Christ. But we can choose to stay home, we can choose not to make the effort, we can choose to do something else. If we choose to worship we can choose any manner or form, formal or informal, in a cathedral or in the church in the wildwood or a thousand variations in between. However we worship, if we worship, we worship directly; we enter personally into the presence of God, we are free to boldly approach the Holy of Holies where God dwells. We are free to experience the presence and the power of God—or not to experience it.

Fourth, there is the implication that we have the freedom to interpret Scripture as guided in our own personal study through the presence of the Holy Spirit. In this we always are suspicious of those who make a claim to be an official interpreter of the Bible, those who say that they have an inside track, and those who say that you have to believe the Bible as they interpret it. This journey is fraught with difficulty. Will D. Campbell is a heroic figure to many in this area of Soul Freedom. Speaking of interpreting the Bible and the many difficult issues we face, he said: "we always take our cue from culture, from Caesar. We discern the signal of culture, rush out and clothe the sight in vague and misinterpreted Scripture, never taking the Bible for what it is, a book about who God is, but as a buttress of the biases of culture. We did it with slavery. We do it with war, gender exclusionism, poverty, and now we're doing it with homophobia."[9]

No, we hold to individuality, the individual and their God, and the Holy Spirit being the line of communication between the two. We study the Scriptures, we read a passage, we pause to reflect on it, we wait for it to infuse itself into our mind and our heart, we test it against the feelings and the experiences which we have, we analyze it, we try to fit it in, we try to hear what it might be saying to us. We seek the advice of other people realizing that we must make up our own mind on its meaning. We study the background trying to put it into the historical context of its time. We look at the Greek and the Hebrew, and occasionally the Aramaic, seeking understanding of what the words mean in other contexts. We open up our commentaries to discern the thinking of those whose life and history is the Scripture. Then we commit ourselves to understanding, always believing that more light or new light might be shed at another time so that we are in a continual process of understanding the meaning of Scripture for our particular time and place.

Baptists, because of their DNA, should be accepting of those who come to another conclusion about their study of the Scripture, for we believe that much in the concept of freedom. In your study you might reject the Scripture, or you might come to a different conclusion about baptism and some of the other doctrines that separate the churches and denominations. However, you have the right and the freedom, indeed, even the responsibility, to form your own conclusions. We may not agree with you. We may challenge you and try to make you see it our way. We may try to convert you. We might dialogue with you with heat and intensity. But the bottom line is your right to seek your own light and understanding, and that is as basic as the "B" in Baptist. Many have died for the principle inherent there.

---

[9] Will D. Campbell, "A Personal Struggle for Soul Freedom," *Christian Ethics Today* (4 December 1995), http://www.christianethicstoday.com.

Finally we each have the freedom to discern the will of God for our own lives. No one else can discern God's will for us. If they say that they can, then run from them. Our guidelines must be our own. The principle is always the same. We must make and be responsible for our own decisions as to what God wants to do with our lives.

As the individual is free, so is the church. We hold dearly to the principle that a local church is free to make and carry out the policies and programs that best reflect and fulfill the purpose that we feel that God has for our church, for education, for personal growth, for worship, for nurture, and for mission. We are guided only by the spirit of Jesus Christ and by our sensitivity to one another, and we must be free to follow the course wherever it might lead us.

Soul Freedom Applied Practically and Personally

I am going to illustrate everything I have said about soul freedom, and to do that I am going to move out on a limb and apply the principle to an issue that is fracturing the church today: homosexuality. If you are saying to yourself, "This guy never takes the easy road" you are correct. But I have your attention! We could be looking at something else that equally divides interpreters but has far less of the visceral and emotional impact of homosexuality, but I choose the difficult road. I tell my students that they have to understand that there are credible Biblical scholars and segments of the Church that sincerely believe that the Bible does not condemn homosexuality, that in fact it allows it as a legitimate, God-given, lifestyle. I tell my students that they do not have to like this, they do not have to believe this, they do not have to accept this; but they do have to understand it because we believe in Soul Freedom. And if they want to discredit it, they have to understand it enough to discredit it rationally, thoughtfully, and with conviction based on their own Scriptural interpretation. Then, even in the midst of dissonance, we move forward together. That is correct, I said *together*. I do not believe, for those of us who are Baptist, there is any other alternative. So, again, I do believe that there is profit for our understanding and our growth with looking at one of the hardest issues of all through the lens of Soul Freedom.

There are two views on the subject of homosexuality that we hear most often. The first says that a homosexual lifestyle is a sin, that it is a violation of, and incompatible with, Scripture. It is here that people can quote chapter and verse. Therefore, a practicing homosexual is living a life of sin outside of and in contradiction to Biblical truth, and that belief and lifestyle of sin must be strongly confronted by the Church. Because of this living outside of Biblical truth, a person who is a homosexual should not be allowed to take a leadership role in the church, nor should they be ordained to the Christian ministry. Churches that violate this Biblical truth should, in like manner, also be excluded from the fellowship of other Baptists. We observe here that people holding this view seem to hold the sin of homosexuality higher in a hierarchy of sins than other transgressions—at least it seems this way to me—for they do not apply the same standards of restraining leadership or stopping fellowship with another church body to other sins that seem to some as equally egregious. Those who hold this view would no doubt hold that sin is sin, and that God does not have a hierarchy in definition or evaluation of it.[10]

A second view says that none of the above is true. This view says that homosexuality is not a choice; it is a fact of creation. This is the way that approximately ten percent of the population is made by God. Those who believe this will go to the Bible and read the same texts and say "we do not interpret them the same way you do; when you read them in context and look at the Bible as a whole there is an allowance for the homosexual lifestyle."

This issue is dividing the wider Church. The Episcopalians are on the verge of schism. The Presbyterians are facing the same situation. The Lutheran Church has a group wanting to split off. The American Baptists have had the secession of a region and numerous churches.

If we Baptists are true to our heritage of Soul Freedom, we should be in the middle saying that you cannot determine the will of God by taking a vote. One of our American Baptist policy statements that condemned homosexuality as incompatible with Scripture and a Christian lifestyle passed by a fifty-two to forty-eight percent vote. We agree that this is democratic, but it is also hurtful to those who interpret the Scripture in a different way and feel that Soul Freedom gives them

---

[10] Reread the article "Church Discipline" in the chapter Regenerate Church Membership and see the comments on 1 Corinthians 5:1–13.

the right of interpretation and freedom to act on that interpretation, believing that this is a God-given Baptist Principle by which we are guided. Soul Freedom does not lend itself to votes; a narrow margin runs roughshod over a strong minority whose only guilt is that they interpreted the Scripture differently.

Soul Freedom says that every individual has the right and the responsibility to search the Scripture and to come to conclusions on what they believe on all such matters. In the end it is likely that we will come to different conclusions on this matter and on a lot of other matters as well. We differ on modes of baptism, we differ on the ordination of women and the role of women in the church, we differ on matters of stewardship, we have differed historically on the matter of slavery—the list goes on.

In the end soul freedom says that I may not agree with you, but I respect your right to make your own personal decision, just as I have the right to make my own personal decision. And most importantly, beyond that, we are bound together by love and by common ministry so we put our differences aside and we work together in love for the common good of the kingdom and the cause of Jesus Christ.

Do you remember the conversation between Jesus and Peter when Jesus asked him, "Who do you say that I am?" (Mk 8:27–30) He did not ask him for a consensus; he asked him for an individual opinion. That is what he asks us. Our responsibility before God is for ourselves, and we must take it seriously, for that is what is meant by Soul Freedom. It is an awesome responsibility that we bear, and for this freedom of faith, we give thanks to God.

Topics for Discussion

Soul Freedom Scenario 1

You are the pastor of an American Baptist Church in Amherst, Massachusetts, which is a college town. You hear from one of the town officials who is a member of your church that the police have taken action against several Jehovah's Witnesses who have been canvassing door-to-door in the neighborhoods. As you speak with this official, the Jehovah's Witnesses are being held in the local jail for violation of local ordinances.

Discussion Questions for Scenario 1

1. Do United States citizens have the right to canvass a neighborhood to sell a product (Avon calling!) or an intangible belief (my version of religious faith)?
2. Do you experience a personal aversion to those who interrupt your daily routine by ringing your doorbell or calling you on the phone?
3. Where or when does solicitation become intrusion?
4. Is this any different from the person who stops you on the street, who wants to explain "God's four spiritual laws" to you or who wants to hand you a tract?
5. Have you ever gone door to door to give people information about your church or about your own personal faith? If not, then why not?
6. What does it mean to: "Go therefore and make disciples of all nations"?[11]
7. What is the Soul Freedom principle here?
8. What is an appropriate response on your part?
9. What action do you take at the close of your conversation? Why do you take it?

Commentary on Scenario 1

This scenario is grounded in my own personal experience. In 1957 I entered the University of Massachusetts in Amherst as a freshman to study chemistry. I was to drop out in the spring of 1958, feeling a call to ministry and wanting to move in another career direction.

While in Amherst, however, I regularly attended the Baptist church there for both morning worship and for a Sunday evening program for the college students. The pastor of that church was the Rev. Doctor Ewald Mann. Following the Second World War, Dr. Mann and his family had come to the United States from Latvia, one of the Slavic countries succumbing to Communism. One Sunday evening he told us this story from the previous week. It had come to his attention that some Jehovah's Witnesses had been knocking on doors in one of the community's neighborhoods, and for their solicitation they had been arrested and

[11] Matthew 28:19, NRSV.

jailed. Dr. Mann said that, "of course, I felt that I had to do something about it." I remember someone asking him what he had done, and his surprised answer, as if it wouldn't be blatantly obvious: "Why I went down and bailed them out!" Then I remember him saying, "I vehemently disagree with everything that they are and everything that they teach, and their intrusive style of knocking on neighborhood doors. But I will die to defend their freedom to come to their own conclusions about faith and to freely practice that faith."

Soul Freedom Scenario 2

A young couple, recently graduated from college, moves into your community and starts attending your church. You are attracted to them because you discover them to be a fine young couple, and you also realize they have leadership gifts that would be very helpful to your church. Invited to their home for a visit, you are told that they are interested in joining your church. Asked about membership requirements, you start first with the church bylaws that require "a profession of Jesus Christ as Savior and Lord." You are caught by their look of dismay, and you are surprised when they say, "we cannot do that." They go on to say that they believe Jesus to be a good man, a son of God, but they have problems with the idea of substitutionary atonement, and the whole idea of "blood washing away our sins." They say that they want to see God as a God of love, not a demanding God with rigid requirements.

Discussion Questions for Scenario 2

1. What is your initial reaction as you listen to them?
2. Should there be a threshold commitment or statement of faith for church membership? What would you accept to be a minimum threshold?
3. Is it possible that, in retrospect, the "half-way covenant"[12] of the early Puritans wasn't such a bad idea after all?
4. What do you say to the couple? Do you tell them that there is no latitude in the membership requirement? Do you "witness" to them about what it is necessary to believe to become a

[12] See the chapter on Regenerate Church Membership.

Christian? Do you take your copy of the four spiritual laws out of your Bible and present it to them? Do you tell them to "fake it," to say it even though they don't believe it. "Lots of people say it without meaning it!" Do you recommend them to the Unitarian-Universalist Church in town?

5. Do you think, "What an exciting opportunity to have them come into our midst and expose them to the heart of our faith, and see them grow as Christians over the years"?
6. Do you tell them that in your church there are a great many people who are at many different points on their faith journey, that it is always changing because people are always changing, and they will find very compatible traveling companions in the life and ministry of your fellowship?
7. What are the parameters of Soul Freedom and Church membership? In other words, how much spread in the concept of faith are you willing to tolerate?
8. Do they need to be expansive? Or restrictive?
9. What is the final action you take on their membership? Why?

Soul Freedom Scenario 3

You are fortunate enough to worship in the ideal Baptist church, one that has figured out a way to encourage wide diversity, living together in common ministry held in tension by differences of opinion in your interpretation of Scripture. So some in your midst believe homosexuality a sin, others do not. Some think abortion is a matter of choice while others do not. Some feel women should be allowed in ministry, others believe the Bible prohibits it.

One day, reality hits. It is not realistic to live in ivory towers of intellectual or spiritual tension. At some point in time, very real situations have to be faced and very real decisions have to be made.

Discussion Questions for Scenario 3

1. In this Church, what guidelines would you use in the real situation of a gay man asking to be ordained?
2. What guidelines would you use if a woman asked for prayer on Sunday morning as she faced an abortion procedure the following week?

3. What guidelines would you use if a lesbian were nominated to be moderator of the Church?
4. How do we transcend intellectual and spiritual commitments within the demands of real life?

Soul Freedom Scenario 4

One Sunday morning, a man worshipping in a Lutheran church rose from his seat, walked out to the narthex, pulled a gun out of his pocket, and shot to death one of the ushers seated at a hospitality table. The man who was shot was a medical doctor who was one of a very small number who would still perform late-term abortions. The man doing the shooting was acting on his belief that all abortion is evil, and the best way to stop abortion is to stop those who are performing them.

It was obvious that the shooting was planned (or premeditated, which is the legal term), and that the shooter would be charged with first-degree murder and convicted, as he has never denied what he did.

In January 2010, as the case was going to trial, the defense asked that the charge be reduced to a much lesser crime, that of voluntary manslaughter. Their argument was that the defendant believed that his action would save unborn children; therefore, it was a positive action that would give life to many in the future. In a stunning development, after deliberation, the judge in the case said that he would allow this kind of argument.

Discussion Questions for Scenario 4

1. What is your initial response after reading this scenario?
2. What do you personally believe about abortion?
3. Is abortion an evil act taking a life or a potential life? Or is abortion a right that every woman has as a matter of free choice? Or could it be both?
4. What is the Biblical case for allowing abortion? Would this be a Soul Freedom issue? Would this also contain elements of Separation of Church and State? If so, then how?
5. What is the Biblical case for not allowing abortion?
6. If you believe that there is a Biblical case against abortion, what does your view do to a woman who believes that Soul

Freedom gives her the right and the freedom to make that decision for herself?

7. Does the Bible speak directly on this matter as with a "Thou shalt ..."?
8. Was the action of the shooter civil disobedience? If it was civil disobedience was it legitimate civil disobedience?
9. Should the shooter pay the harshest penalty allowable for his civil disobedience act or should he be made into an icon of conscience? Does the "purity" of his motive make a difference in your thinking and judgment? Would you give that same act of choice in making a decision to the abortion doctor, allowing him to perform the abortion?
10. Do you believe that a death that gives life to others is a justifiable death?
11. Would you feel any differently if this had happened in your church?
12. Would you feel any differently if you had known week after week the abortion doctor as a fellow church member?
13. Would you feel any differently if you had known the shooter?

Soul Freedom Scenario 5

In 2009, California voters passed a ban on gay and lesbian marriage, making such unions unbinding and removing any legal status to them. This overturned what had been in place in parts of the state, notably San Francisco where marriages were approved for a time, and ceremonies were actively performed.

In January 2010, a lesbian couple and a gay couple adjudicated in the California court attempting to overturn the action of the voters. Said one of the lesbian plaintiffs, "You chose them (your partner) over everybody else, and you want to feel that it is going to stick and that you are going to have the protection and support and inclusion that comes from letting people know you feel that way."[13]

To the consternation of many who oppose gay marriage, the lawyer for the plaintiffs has very conservative credentials, having served in the

---

[13] Associated Press, "Questions abound in gay marriage trial," *The Indianapolis Star*, 12 January 2010.

Office of legal Counsel under Ronald Reagan, and as the Solicitor General for George W. Bush.[14] In speaking of this case he says that he "believes in individual liberty and freedom from government interference in the private lives of citizens. Discriminating against people because of sexual orientation is a violation of both."[15]

Discussion Questions for Scenario 5

1. What is your initial reaction to reading this scenario?
2. Are you one who has a visceral, emotional reaction when people talk positively about gay and lesbian marriage?
3. Do you believe that gay and lesbian marriage should be a Soul Freedom issue? What about a Biblical Authority issue? Is there a difference if it is one or the other? Is there a difference if it is both/and?
4. Are there some areas beyond the reach of, or off limits to, Soul Freedom judgments?
5. What do you think about the statement by the plaintiff's attorney about "individual liberty and freedom?" Do you feel the same way? If you do, do you feel it all of the time or only to certain issues?
6. If you differentiate on the issues of freedom, what is your standard of differentiation? Why do you think it applies to this issue and not others? Or why do you think it does not apply to this issue, but does to others?
7. What do you think of this statement: "In the words of the highest court in the land, marriage is the most important relationship in life and of fundamental importance to all individuals."[16] Do you agree or disagree with that above statement?
8. This statement was used by the plaintiff's attorney in support of their right to marriage. Does that change how you think about it?

---

[14] Eve Conan, "The Conscience of a Conservative," *Newsweek Magazine* (18 January 2010): 47.

[15] Ibid.

[16] Associated Press, ["Questions abound in gay marriage trial,"] *The Indianapolis Star,* 12 January 2010. The quote is from a decision handed down by the United States Supreme Court.

9. Would having a gay or lesbian member in your family change your view on the topic?

Soul Freedom Scenario 6

You are a new minister in town, and one of your active church members asks for an appointment to see you. It turns out that he is a member of the local Rotary Club, and he thinks that your belonging would be good for you, for the church, and for the community at large. He offers to introduce your name for membership and to pay your dues for the first several years.

After joining and attending your first several meetings you realize that there is a subplot at work. Although there is a category for ministers in Rotary, from a practical standpoint they are there to give the prayer as the meeting opens. There are very few members who are comfortable praying in public, and after all, praying is part of a minister's job.

You pray, and you end your prayer as you customarily do in church, "in the name of Jesus Christ Our Lord, Amen."

As you are going out your church member slaps you on the back and says "thank you" for the way that you bore witness to the Lordship of Jesus Christ in your prayer.

Later you hear from one of the other members—very discreetly—that a friend of his, a Jewish professional man, was offended to the reference to Jesus Christ. He felt that he was being "preached to" and that he certainly was not included in the prayer. The prayer was not speaking to him. He did not feel that the Rotary Club was the appropriate place for such a prayer.

As you think about it, and talk to others, you find that there are at least two main views on this issue. The first says that ministers praying in public should be bold about their faith, and use the opportunity to bring the gospel message to those who are there, believing that the Holy Spirit might plant the seeds of a future conversion. The second says that Rotary is not a church, that by praying you take on the office of representing a multiplicity of religious views, and that your prayer should reflect that diversity with a nonsectarian closing.

You wonder if closing in the "name of the God of Abraham, Isaac and Jacob" would be more inclusive. Some would feel that would satisfy both the Jewish and Christian members who were actually paying attention to what you were saying. Of course your most conservative church member would want to bring you back to specifically witnessing to a saving faith. And your solution still doesn't accommodate those who do not fit into the Christian-Jewish box.

Others suggest to you that even the Jewish/Christian ending is too confining, that your prayer should embrace all of the "religious" elements present in a pluralistic society, and perhaps even the totally non-sectarian Rotarian, of which, no doubt, there are a few.

Discussion Questions for Scenario 6

1. What does it mean to do ministry in a pluralistic environment?
2. What is the tension between "bearing witness" and respecting the principle of Soul Freedom, the right of others to make their own religious opinions for themselves, and for you to honor those decisions?
3. Would you consider this kind of prayer a badgering of others, beating them over the head with your religious stick? Would you accept the fact that there would be some who did feel this? How would you respond to this alternative viewpoint?
4. Would you feel any different if it was the Muslim Imam who gave the prayer each meeting day and you were the one subject to his evangelism?
5. Isn't your life, your conversation, your decisions, your bearing, your personhood, sufficient witness as to who and what you are and all that for which you stand?
6. What is the meaning of what is called "friendship evangelism," that of witnessing through friendship and involvement as opposed to "preaching" in such situations?
7. What kinds of questions about all of this are going through your mind?
8. What would you do in situations such the Rotary Club or other such situations?

Commentary on Scenario 6

I have lived on both sides of this issue, and it is one of the issues on which I have changed my mind. Early in my ministerial career I felt that as an ordained minister, called by God to bear witness to my faith, I needed always to be authentic to whom I was. With that in mind, I would end my prayers "in the name of Jesus Christ." To any argument, I would simply say, "Well, they knew who I was when they asked me!"

As I grew older and had the opportunity to move into more public settings, I began to believe that in certain circumstances I was being asked to pray on behalf of a more diverse group, and that my prayer should reflect that diversity. With that I would simply say "Amen" at the conclusion of the prayer.

For many years I served on the board of Franklin College, a college with Baptist roots located in Franklin, Indiana. Naturally I was asked to pray at the beginning of board meetings, for lunches, for convocations, for graduation ceremonies, and on those occasions I simply closed with an "Amen." There were a number of occasions when a member of the faculty and/or staff approached me at the conclusion and thanked me for my respecting their tradition and not "forcing" my own upon them. I felt at the time that they knew full well who I was, that they knew the options I had before me, and so I did not feel that I had given up anything in being inclusive, that indeed I had gained some good will to foster better future relationships.

This has been a public matter in the Indianapolis press in recent years. The legislature (house and senate) was taken to court by civil libertarians to stop the strong sectarian prayers that were opening the house and senate sessions. Some were respectful of the multiple traditions in both the state and the governing body; others felt it appropriate to "preach" a strong message of faith and some of those prayers became sermons.

The United States District Court for the Southern District of Indiana, upholding previous actions it cited by the United States Supreme Court, issued an injunction against sectarian prayers in legislative sessions, citing the issue of the "establishment of religion." Predictably, depending on viewpoint, this has ruling has been both blessed and vilified.

Of interest, the federal judge who gave the ruling, David Hamilton, was recently appointed to the Seventh Circuit Court of Appeals, and when his name came before Congress for approval, there was strong opposition from those who felt that his decision for denying sectarian prayer was in error. His detractors did not prevail, and Hamilton's appointment received sufficient votes for passage.

It should be recognized that there are, and will continue to be, very strong opinions on both sides of this issue.

Soul Freedom Scenario 7

(Also: Separation of Church and State Also Civil Disobedience)

In the mid nineteenth century, the Commonwealth of Massachusetts subjected citizens who were eligible to vote to a poll tax, meaning that in order to vote they would have to register and pay a tax. There were some who felt that the ballot was a privilege and obligation of citizenship, and that the poll tax was unconstitutional in that it prohibited many members from voting solely because of their financial situation.

There were those who protested—one is reminded of the culture that a century before had thrown chests of tea into Boston Harbor in protest of another tax upon the colonialists.

One of those who took exception to the tax was the popular naturalist and writer Henry David Thoreau. For him, the tax was an issue of conscience, a violation of principle and right, and this conscience and right demanded that he forcefully stand for his principles in protest. For that protest and the manner of it he was put into jail where he languished, unwilling to pay bail for something that he felt was an inalienable right: i.e. civil disobedience before the established government.

It is said that the famous philosopher and poet Ralph Waldo Emerson visited Thoreau in jail, greeting him with "Henry, what are you doing in here?" To which Thoreau answered, "Ralph, what are you doing out there?"

Discussion Questions for Scenario 7

1. What resonance does this story strike with you?
2. What is the nature of civil disobedience?
3. Where are its roots in Baptist Principles?
4. Should civil disobedience be allowed without penalty?
5. If there are penalties, how severe or restrictive should they be?
6. Do we have to pay a price for God given rights?
7. What does it mean to be subject to the civil authorities?
8. How do you equate this with Martin Luther King and the march on Birmingham? The Berrigan Brothers breaking into Selective

Service records and pouring blood on them? A gunman shooting an abortion doctor?

9. Where do you see in current public life some areas where you think that civil disobedience might be appropriate?

Soul Freedom Scenario 8
(Also: Biblical Authority)

After 9/11, Jerry Falwell made a statement about the terrorist attack and the reasons behind his judgment. He said: "I really believe that the pagans and the abortionists and the feminists and the gays and the lesbians who are actively trying to make that an alternative lifestyle—all of them who have tried to secularize America—I point the finger in their face and say, 'You helped this happen.'" A later column on the editorial page of the *Indianapolis Star* pointed out that if you believed this, then it was because of these people that God removed the wall of protection from thousands of Americans drinking their morning coffee in the twin towers and in the Pentagon. The column went on to say of Falwell, "What better spokesman for the Taliban? Our fundamentalists agree with theirs. God is on their side. America's sins are to blame."[17]

Discussion Questions for Scenario 8

1. What is your initial reaction as you read this account of 9/11?
2. What are the individual and distinctive Baptist Principles at play here?
3. Does Soul Freedom give Falwell the right to think, believe, and say what he said in a public statement?
4. What do you think of the person who said that we should "beware of those who believe that they have the right to speak judgment on God's behalf"? What do you think this person is trying to say?
5. Does God judge us by having airplanes fly into buildings? Or sending earthquakes to Haiti? Or Tsunamis to Indonesia? Or getting cancer?
6. Why would Falwell's catalogue of sins be any more deserving of punishment than others?

---

[17] Ellen Goodman, *The Baltimore Sun*, September 23, 2001.

7. At work the next morning several have seen this article on Falwell and they ask your opinion of it. What do you tell them? Do you tell them that sometimes it is not easy being a Baptist? (Think of how this can be interpreted two different and opposite ways.)
8. Do you agree with me when I suggest that, every time I see or hear a religious commentary that I consider to be "off the wall" and "nowhere in the realm of reasoned thoughtfulness," it always turns out to be a vituperative comment by someone identifying as a Baptist? (I know, I know, it's the price of Soul Freedom!)

Commentary on Scenario 8

These words were written in the aftermath of the deadly January 2010 earthquake that devastated the island of Haiti, exacerbating the terrible suffering of one of the poorest nations on earth. One of the more controversial comments to come out of this was made by Pat Robertson on his religious program *The 700 Club*. He said that when they were looking for freedom from France, Haitians made a pact with Satan, a pact that pledged obedience to Satan for freedom. Robertson went on to say that the earthquake was God's judgment for that pact. We note that Robertson did not give specifics as to how he knew this had happened, he did not bring forth any documents, he did not call forth any witnesses, he simply made a statement of what he felt was fact. Do we assume that he has a line to heaven that none of us have where he learns God's will without our being able to have a verification process? Or even a discussion about it? No, he simply states it as true.

Curiously, the outpouring from across the United States was uniform in condemning Robertson for his comments, and the condemnation came from a wide religious, and non-religious, spectrum. One writer even brought forth a different view with a letter from Satan himself, reminding us of C.S. Lewis and his *Screwtape Letters*:

> Dear Pat Robertson, I know that you know that all press is good press, so I appreciate the shout-out. And you make God look like a big mean bully who kicks people when they are down, so I'm all over that action. But when you say that Haiti has made a pact with me, it is totally humiliating. I may be evil incarnate, but I'm no welcher. The

> way you put it, making a deal with me leaves folks desperate and impoverished. Sure, in the afterlife, but when I strike bargains with people, they first get something here on earth—glamour, beauty, talent, wealth, fame, glory, a golden fiddle. Those Haitians have nothing, and I mean nothing. And that was before the earthquake.[18]

The response opinions that we saw showed us that the United States is not yet devoid of religious faith, and that some of that religious faith is careful, thoughtful, and creatively expressive. We do not like those who would try to speak, especially irresponsibly, on our behalf seeking to interpret world events, and the mind or will of God.

Again, we are wary of those who tell us that they are speaking on God's behalf. At the same time, we defend with every breath their Soul Freedom right to have such an opinion and to express it freely.

Soul Freedom Scenario 9[19]

(Also: Biblical Authority and Autonomy of the Local Church)

A college town church is dually aligned with the United Church of Christ and the American Baptist Churches, USA. Over the course of a year, with due process, the UCC side of the church approves the ordination to Christian ministry of a gay man who openly professes his homosexuality. After the ordination, the churches in the local Baptist Association to which the church belongs on its Baptist side begin to circulate a petition calling for the removal of the hand of fellowship from that church. The church is stunned by this action; as a local Baptist church they had done, in their estimation, nothing wrong. The ordination and all of its proceedings and actions was in the hand of what would amount to the local United Church of Christ. The members of the association circulating the petition are undaunted by this argument; they are guilty by association. They never should have allowed the issue to move forward, and when it did they should have removed themselves from the alliance, seeking unity with those whose interpretations of the Bible mirrored those of the Baptist Association.

---

[18] Robert Schlesinger, "The Devil Responds to Pat Robertson on Haiti," Thomas Jefferson St. Blog, *US News and World Report*, 16 January 2010.

[19] This scenario is also found in the chapter on The Autonomy of the Local Church, Scenario 3.

Discussion Questions for Scenario 9

1. What is your initial reaction to this situation as you read about it?
2. What/where are the Baptist Principles in this unfolding story?
3. Where are these principles present? Where are they absent? Where are they abused? Where are they misinterpreted?
4. Does the church body have a right of collective Soul Freedom to make a decision on how they are going to view the subject of homosexuality?
5. Does the association have the right to draw lines concerning who can be in the fellowship and who cannot be in it?
6. Do you think that this action of the association was harsh, or do you think that this action was courageous? On what basis do you hold your view?
7. Can you clearly state what the opposing view was (the one you were against) and why some people would have stood with it?
8. Do you think the church had a point in arguing that this was not the Baptist Church but their sister UCC church that made the decision, and they should not be judged guilty by it? Or would you judge them guilty by complicity as well?
9. Could you justify the action of the Association in the Biblical warnings to those who would be a stumbling block to others in the faith?[20]

[20] We would note the following: Mark 9:42, where Jesus speaks of children, and says that for any that would be a stumbling block to them, it would be better for them to have a millstone around their neck and thrown into the sea; Romans 11:9, where Paul admonishes that a stumbling block or hindrance should never be put in the way of another; 1 Corinthians 8:9, where Paul admonishes that Christians should be careful that their liberty never become a stumbling block to the Jews.

Soul Freedom Scenario 10[21]

(Also: Biblical Authority and Autonomy of the Local Church)

The local Baptist Association did eventually vote to remove the hand of fellowship from the Baptist church in question (see Soul Freedom Scenario 9), arguing that they could not be in fellowship with a church complicit in such an event they deemed biblically wrong. Under the standards of the American Baptist Churches, USA, the disfellowshiped church had two years to join another association. The executive director of a local region that was contiguous to the disfellowshiping region initiated dialogue, inviting the church to join its association. That started several months of very painful discussion within the inviting association, and it became quickly evident that many of the association ministers and churches did not share the view of their executive. The arguments landed on traditional sides, an open interpretation of Scripture versus a more legalistic view of Scripture and a holiness view of separation from that which in their eyes would be an abomination before God. In the end, the association board had a majority in favor, but fell short of a two-thirds vote necessary for welcoming a new church into the association, and the local church was told that it would have to find another region with which they could unite.

Discussion Questions for Scenario 10

1. What/where are the Baptist Principles in this unfolding story? Where are they present? Where are they absent? Where are they abused? Where are they misinterpreted?
2. In your judgment, how does a denomination or an association deal with pluralism—that is, dealing with groups of individuals who interpret the Scripture differently on certain contentious matters? Is there any way through this?
3. Does Soul Freedom have limits?
4. Does Biblical Authority have limits?

---

[21] This scenario is also found in the chapter on The Autonomy of the Local Church, Scenario 3.

Commentary on Scenario 10

This experience is written as it happened. Though it was almost a decade ago, the memory of those times seems fresh. Sad to say, in some instances, in some places, in some relationships there is still pain and brokenness. There are relationships that fractured in these meetings, and they have never healed. In other relationships there is distrust and a shift in the spirit of fellowship and camaraderie. As a people who claim Biblical faith, we do not always do well with forgiveness and reconciliation.

In the end, the disfellowshiped church did find another region. In the region where the vote was taken not to receive the disfellowshiped church, two churches left of their own accord. These were churches that strongly disagreed with allowing the disfellowshiped church to join—in other words, these two churches won the vote. We can only speculate that they left simply because the question was entertained and such entertainment exceeded their tolerance levels.

So, on this very important matter, we could not agree to disagree. It is one of those instances of which we spoke above where Biblical Authority trumped Soul Freedom, where a single biblical view on a subject did not allow any differences in Scriptural interpretation. The Soul Freedom of the offending church was not given any credence at all.

3

The Autonomy of the Local Church

The Autonomy of the Local Church is one of our Baptist Principles. By "autonomy" we mean that there is no influence, governance and/or control, no hierarchy of power, outside of, or over, the life of the congregation. The authority, the governance of that local church rests solely within the congregation itself. Each Baptist church is independent or self-contained, answering to no higher authority.

We see this Autonomy of the Local Church as an extension of the idea of Soul Freedom. Soul Freedom asserts that each person in relationship to God through the saving grace of Jesus Christ is empowered and expected, required in fact, to individually nurture that relationship, and to discover in God's revelation to us the guidelines and truths which are to shape and form our lives. Thus through prayer, through reading the Scriptures, through dialogue with other believers, we arrive, often with struggle and difficulty, at conclusions that become the guiding and nurturing source of our existence. With this we are on a journey of discovery, gaining new understanding and application of God's truth revealed to us. The mystery of God as it is revealed to us for the living of our lives is never exhausted.

As individuals of faith we join together in covenant to form the local church, and the solitary process that forms us as individuals in search for personal truth multiplies into the corporate foundation of the life and ministry to be shared together. Now instead of one we are many striving through prayer, dialogue, and study to discern God's will and truth for the wider focus of our lives to be at work in the world. To give ourselves to an outside structure or authority in determining those decisions and direction would be a violation of the very purposes that brought us together.

Like the individual believer, each corporate group of believers formed into a church would affirm the lordship of Jesus Christ over their life, their lives, and their common mission and ministry. We will speak more on this in the section on the Biblical basis for the Autonomy of the Local Church.

Each local church, through a congregational process, will give authority to its leadership; this would include pastors, deacons, trustees, and teachers—anyone in fact who is a leader, if not a decision-maker, within the structure. This authority will set any needed limits on what the leadership can or cannot do. It also states clearly who can be a member of the church, the process by which one becomes a member, the prerequisite faith and commitment statement needed for membership, the responsibilities and requirements of membership, matters related to budgets, investments, and financial oversight, and acquisition and maintenance of property and buildings.

Biblical Basis for the Autonomy of the Local Church

With the Bible clearly stated as the source of our authority (see Biblical Authority), it is important for us as Baptists to find our structure based on autonomy in the New Testament Church, for modeling this New Testament Church is crucial to our sense of identity and purpose.

Baptist Biblical scholars will commonly identify the following Scriptures as promoting autonomy in the church described in the pages of the New Testament, with these practices a model and example for our own structure:

Matthew 18:15–17: This passage has to do with conflict between two members of the church. To resolve the conflict, the person wronged first is to approach the person who sinned against them; if that fails they are to bring one or two others to seek resolution, and if that fails they are to bring the matter before the church. It is pointed out that all of this takes place within the confines of the local church and there is no outside individual or authority to be brought in to compel a resolution or compliance.

Acts 6:1–7: This passage speaks of a problem related to rapid growth within the early church. As the numbers were increasing and the leadership was increasingly attempting to meet the needs of all, the Hellenists complained that their widows were not receiving a fair amount of food in the daily distribution. The leadership said that they did not feel that they should neglect the proclamation of the gospel to "wait on tables" (Acts 6:2) and so it was that seven men were chosen to meet these needs of distribution so that none would be neglected. Again there is no mention of outside authority or intervention; it was a problem for the church and it was handled within the structure of that local church.

Acts 13:1–3, 14:26–27: In the chapter thirteen verses, Paul and Barnabas were sent off on a missionary journey by the church in Antioch, and in the fourteenth chapter they give a report to that very same church upon their return. These missionaries were appointed solely by the local Antioch church and were responsible to that church when they reported back.

1 Corinthians 5:1–13: Here, Paul is speaking of issues within the life of the church at Corinth—sexual immorality, boasting, associating with immoral persons—and he makes clear what he thinks the proper response and action should be by the members of the church. We note however, that he is not dictatorial, stating what must take place. He speaks, instead, out of his own heart and experience, and he seeks to *persuade* them to do the right thing, a far stretch from *demanding* that they do the right thing. He has the moral authority of an apostle, but he does not claim that as authority and power to force something upon the church. Whatever happens will happen solely within the life and action of that church.

Acts 4:18–20, 5:29: In this passage, the Jerusalem authorities are attempting to silence Peter and John as they proclaim the gospel and bring people into a faith in Jesus Christ. Peter and John were ordered by the authorities to stop their evangelistic effort, a request they refused, stating clearly that: "we cannot keep from speaking about what we have seen and heard" (Acts 4:20). In the second passage, the authorities arrest Peter and the disciples for their healing and preaching work in the temple; they are taken to jail and imprisoned, and miraculously released by an angel of God. Again they are called before the council and told to stop, and again they proclaim that: "We must obey God rather than any human authority" (Acts 5:29). Through all this runs the belief that individual and church freedom dismisses any outside authority over the conviction of process, and the action that comes from the discernment of God's Word and will through the guidance of the Holy Spirit.

The Effectiveness and Efficiencies of Interdependence

Baptists learned early that while their belief in Soul Freedom extended into independence and autonomy for the local church, there were efficiencies—and effectiveness—in banding together into organizational structures with other like-minded churches. Thus we have the birth of Baptist associations on the local level, and denominations on the wider level.

These wider organizations could make things happen with a facility that the smaller local church could not. The covenantal relationship was always voluntary, and the authority given to the wider church was marginal and limited. These areas of expanded work and ministry might include:

Missions: Local churches might not have the resources to hire missionaries and send them across to globe in keeping with the mandate of Jesus Christ to proclaim the gospel to all nations. Pooling our resources, however, a national organization representing several thousand churches can create a support structure that can easily do this on behalf of many. We might note that in 1813, when Luther Rice returned from Burma, he traversed the eastern reaches of a growing United States, bringing the churches together to support the missional enterprise. When the first Triennial Convention met in 1814, it was founded to move forward in support of Adoniram and Ann Judson, and the other missionaries who would soon follow. Our Baptist denominations were founded as advocates for the global proclamation of the Gospel in fulfillment of the mandate of Jesus to "Go into all of the world" (Mt 28:16-20).

Publications: A denomination has the wider resources to develop church school curriculum, to publish Bibles, Bible commentaries and other biblical study references, to define and interpret history, and to prepare devotional material to encourage reflection and inspiration. There is also room for a wider diversity of thought and dialogue, which we would interpret favorably, for diversity is in a sense a sharpening stone against which we hone our individual thoughts and reflections towards meeting the needs of our personal and corporate lives. (The author takes the view that unanimity at all times is both dull and boring and, at times, unproductive for creative thinking. Many, he knows, would disagree, desiring unanimity at all costs.)

Public witness: We believe that we are, individually and collectively, called to be prophetic within the society at large, that we are to be leaven at work, bearing witness to the meaning of our faith and, as we see it, its application to the life that we live together. Again, pooling resources gives us a larger voice and a bigger platform; our problem, with our Baptist diversity, is that there are Baptists on every side of every issue. Soul Freedom leads us to many different conclusions, and freedom brings differing conclusions based on the same data. We cite, for example, different interpretations as to what the Bible allows on the subjects of divorce, slavery, women in ministry, abortion, and homosexuality. Nevertheless, where there is, after prayer and discussion, consensus and/or even unanimity, then that must be proclaimed, in the prophetic image of a plumb bob measuring truth against the life within the societies in which we live. And at the very least, conscience would call us to have a public dialogue, heart to heart, mind to mind within the space where we must live together in the peace of Jesus Christ, even in the midst of our differences, especially in the midst of our differences. We must note that such statements of proclamation are just that; they are not mandates, for a mandate would cross the line of autonomy. This is a very fine difference, but we create enormous difficulties for ourselves when we believe them to be mandates, when we insist on them being mandates. They can never be more than opinions, grist for the mill of dialogue, looking for discernment, one cog in the wheel of moving forward.

Membership movement: The State of Maine has small fishing villages along its coast, small farming communities inland, and it is covered with a vast forest housing communities of those who work in the woods. Maine historians teach us that there was a large exodus from Maine after the Civil War as land opened up in the west; the vast fertile plains looked like heaven to those who had broken their plows in Maine's rocky soil. As these farmers moved west, they would ask for a letter of commendation from the church to which they belonged. Such letters would testify that they were members in good standing of that church, that they were people of faith, that they had been active in the life of that church. This meant that when they arrived in the new territories and started to build their new homes, churches, and communities, they had a document that identified them, so they weren't starting from scratch. It became a common practice, in starting a new church, to accept these letters, so that individuals could build on who they had been, who they were, and not have to begin their faith journey anew. It was very important, for example, that a former baptism be recognized. For one thing, such recognition greatly simplified the transfer to a new place, as a re-baptism would not be required. But it also kept baptism from being merely a ritual of church membership, instead recognizing that when baptism follows our declaration of faith in Jesus Christ, it becomes part of the most important transformational event of our lives, an event that can never be duplicated. Baptism without transformation becomes pro forma, a duty with little meaning. We see this idea of transfer with many of the Burmese refugees who are coming to our shores today. Brought up in Burma in the church birthed by God through the ministry of Adoniram Judson and the countless missionaries who followed him there, these refugees often seek out American Baptist Churches as they come to the United States, or at least Baptist churches, for there they know they will be home, recognized and honored for the faith and church that has shaped their lives in their homeland.

Ordination: We must stress the fact that every ordination is a local ordination. It is the local church that entertains the possibility that an individual has a call to ministry. It is the local church that ascertains the sense of call and the presence of skills needed in ministry, and it is the local church that sets the individual aside with laying on of hands. In many instances national denominations have created standards for ordination, and unless those standards are met they will not recognize an ordination. What that means is that they will not open their resources to help with placement. In the Baptist tradition, the individual is ordained in the local church, and the denomination cannot take that away. In the local church there is the recognition that a national system helps with movement among churches, that one church knows as they interview a candidate that the individual has undergone a recognition process that lets the interviewing church know up front that certain things about the individual being considered are true, that there is a history to be examined, and that they do not have to start from scratch. Working together, we do not have to start over every time we move to a new church; we can recognize a person's history and accept the judgment and actions of others who have gone on before us. To be clear, a person not recognized by the national body for whatever reason, but ordained by the local church, is still considered ordained in the eyes of the church. Their only limitation would be the lack of movement beyond that congregation without going through the entire ordination process with another church.

Fellowship: This is simply to say that we have learned that there is great value in meeting together in large denominational groups. There is a great joy, the presence often of the Holy Spirit, as we lift our hearts and voices together in worship, in study, in deliberation, in preaching, in prayer.

The Troublesome Aspects of Autonomy

There is, we all know, a terrible price to freedom, and we see it play out when an individual or a group of individuals use their freedom to destroy themselves or others. Even God had a problem with the price of freedom as we read in Genesis 6:5–6: "The Lord saw that the wickedness of humankind was great in the earth, and that every inclination of the thoughts of their hearts was only evil continually. And the Lord was sorry that he had made humankind on the earth, and it grieved him to his heart." It was at this point that God wanted to destroy all that had been created.

Or there is the familiar story of the prodigal son who, given his freedom and a purse, squanders it all recklessly. Or there is the older brother who has it all, but who chooses instead to be petulant, judgmental, and vindictive. Unfortunately we all know of individuals who fit in either category, who have shamelessly dissipated the incredible freedom given to them by God. That is the risk that is given with the gift.

So it is, in freedom, that a church divides over an issue, and the "wrong group" maintains control of the building and the assets so that they are lost to a region or a denomination, whereas, in a hierarchical structure, the assets would stay with the denomination, the true and the faithful (the winners are always the true and the faithful).

So, a church in its freedom calls an individual to be its pastor and everyone knows that the individual is not loyal to the denomination and has numerous faults that are going to hurt or destroy the church and its mission. Freedom has within it inherent self-destruction, and we are amazed at how often individuals and groups head down that slippery slope.

Looking another way, we see that while freedom is a church issue, responsibility for what we do with this freedom remains with the individual. Often we use our own standards to categorize individuals, judging them to be unlike us. We use pious words such as "Biblical" or "spiritual" to describe ourselves, while telling others that they are unlike us and that the standards we have created are absolute. All of this is to insist that they conform to our standards, sometimes with the caveat that failure to do so will put their life, or their soul, or their salvation in dire jeopardy. What we learn from our belief in freedom or autonomy is that, if we are truly Baptist, we have to allow others, to make their choices in spite of the consequences, meanwhile standing by, even as the father of the prodigal son did, to welcome them home if ever they should come to their senses. It is the great irony of Biblical faith that the first is last and the last is first, where sometimes everything may be upside down and out of kilter, the shoe may be on the other foot and we may need to come to our senses and return home. It may be us who must realize the error of our ways and seek to come back. It works both ways. Keeping options open, continuing to dialogue, living in love and grace, allows diversity to be redemptive.

Just as no one can tell us how or what to believe, or how to interpret Scripture, so does it follow that we cannot tell another individual or another Baptist Church what to believe. We can challenge them, we can argue with them, and we can dialogue with them, but in the end we cannot make them conform to a singular view (our singular view)—this is contrary to all that we believe. We can legitimately break the bond of fellowship with them, but the loss in doing that is enormous, for diversity is the stimulus to probing into Scripture for deeper understandings. Differences of opinion sharpen our focus, our understanding, and finally, our life.

I remember the great frustration of the General Secretary of the American Baptist Churches in the midst of recent disagreements of what a Biblical understanding of homosexuality might be. Even though it was a power he did not have, he was under great pressure to "discipline" recalcitrant churches to "bring them to heel" by forcing or threatening disfellowship. Many of these individuals did not understand that the price of freedom is diversity, differences of opinion, very strong differences of opinion, and even fracturing differences of opinion at times. Nevertheless, living within that tension and diversity and disagreement is who we are. It is the Baptist way, and in the end it makes us strong. But it has the possibility to make the journey a hell on earth.

The Priesthood of the Individual Believer and Autonomy

We would surely want to make the additional point here that our Baptist Principle of the Priesthood of the Individual Believer lends credence to our belief in the Autonomy of the Local Church. As priests, with individual responsibility to act on our own behalf and on behalf of others, we have direct access to God with no intermediary necessary. That is another impetus to join together with others of like mind in the journey of faith, participating in the fellowship and governance of the church seeking through prayer and the guidance of the Holy Spirit the truth and direction of ministry and mission. Such would not tolerate anything other than autonomy.

Topics for Discussion

Autonomy of the Local Church Scenario 1

The regional executives of a major Baptist denomination call a meeting. At issue is the placement of pastors. Many churches are calling pastors who prove to be destructive to the church's involvement in denominational life. This means a diminishing of regional resources as the church allocates its mission dollars elsewhere; it sometimes means the loss of assets to the denomination; it always means the destruction of personal ties that might have taken years to develop. The answer for the executives is to reclassify the regional executive office to that of a Bishop, with the Bishop having the powers of pastoral appointment and removal. They feel that pragmatism and retention of the status quo demands a shift from traditional Baptist Principle.

Discussion Questions for Scenario 1

1. What do you think is going on here?
2. Would you entertain their motion, thinking that it might have merit? If so, why?

3. Or are you utterly aghast, hardly able to believe that Baptist leaders would call for dissolution of sacredly held principles? If so, why?
4. Is the argument about assets and their retention specious? Or does it have merit? Would the value of the assets make a difference? For example a large building vs. a small building? A piece of property consisting of large acreage? An endowment fund of many millions of dollars or one with no assets?
5. Do the assets of any Baptist church ever belong to the denomination?
6. Is this a good example of the idea that freedom can be troublesome? If yes, why? If no, why?

Autonomy of the Local Church Scenario 2

There is something amiss in your local Baptist church, and you find yourself increasingly uncomfortable. The issue is a decision or decisions made in church meetings that you feel are not true to Scripture and ministry as you interpret it through your own life of study, prayer, and reflection. It could be a building project that you feel would severely tax the resources of the congregation, diverting those resources from programs and areas that you feel to be crucial to ministry. It could be a statement of inclusion, saying that gays and lesbians are more than welcome to be involved in the active life of the church. Or it could be a statement of exclusion saying that homosexuality is a sin and that gays and lesbians are not welcome in the life of the congregation unless they repent and give up their sinful lifestyle. It could be a decision to give the congregation's support to a political candidate because of their support for beliefs held by a majority of the church. You consider the following options:

<u>Option one</u>: You wonder if you should leave, and seek another church. You realize that this decision is dependent on your level of comfort; how angry or disappointed are you at the decisions that have been made. Are they game changers? Part of the decision would have to do with the involvement of your family; are they invested in parts of the church that make it very difficult for them to move on? At the same time you are aware of the fact that you could move into another church with a certain degree of anonymity, go to worship on Sunday morning, and

limit your involvement to no more than that. This would be satisfying on some level, but not so satisfying on another, but it is a choice. This in fact, would be true of all three options.

Option two: You could become a church dropout. Whether your family joins you or not, this is what you are going to do. You are going to schedule those weekend trips that you have longed to take, but sometimes felt your church responsibilities would not allow. Or you are going to find a place to walk on Sunday morning and feel God's presence in the world around you. Or you are going to join one of those leagues—play or coach—that have had the temerity to have previously excluded you by playing on Sunday morning. (In fact you are somewhat surprised at the number of activities going on—you have never noticed them because you have always been busy on Sunday mornings.)

Option three: You decide to stay with it. Part of your decision is rationalization. You think to yourself, "The problem is, such a move takes an extraordinary amount of energy." If you are connected within the life of the church the loss of personal relationship is extremely painful. You lose a measure of comfort—after all, you have attended that church for a number of years and you are familiar with it, its people, its ways of operation, its pluses and minuses, faults and advantages, failures and successes. You realize that you might have differences within institution, that no organization or fellowship is without its imperfections. Better the ones that you know than the ones that you don't. But beyond the rationalization, you come to a profound discovery, realizing that the very nature of being Baptist often leads beyond dialogue to contention. In other words, being a real Baptist demands hard work in the discernment process of study, prayer, and dialogue, and because other people have that same freedom, the probability of dissension is one hundred percent. With that you realize that such periods of dissention are the very times when you have been forced to grow in your faith, to return to the Scripture for deeper study, to broaden your horizons of prayer, to approach dialogue and discussion with far more serious intent. Living in a covenantal community, whether a marriage, church, workplace, town or city, means that there always is going to be dialogue and intentionality to work through and differences that are bound to divide us. In the end we may discover that this is the reason God gave us love and grace in abundance—a fact for which we are grateful when we encounter those times when we need every bit.

Discussion Questions for Scenario 2

1. If we are Baptists, truly Baptists, why is option two not an option at all?
2. What is wrong with option one if you are a Baptist with strong autonomy convictions? In other words, can a Baptist be in the life of a church without being deeply involved in its life and ministry? Isn't everything we are and believe predicated on active involvement? Discuss this.
3. What are the thresholds that would actually make you consider leaving and finding another church?
4. An older gentlemen, who was a long time Baptist and participant in numerous Baptist dialogues, when asked about his life of faith said colloquially, "Being a Baptist ain't for sissies!" What do you think he meant by that? What is it about being a Baptist that requires discipline, commitment, and hard work?
5. Would you consider option three an idealist statement from the author of this book? What is your reaction to it?

Autonomy of the Local Church Scenario 3[1]

Part One: A college town church is dually aligned with the United Church of Christ and the American Baptist Churches, USA; both of these denominations have a history of strong independence and autonomy within the local church. Over the course of a year, with due process, the UCC side of the church approves and carries out the ordination to Christian ministry of a gay man who openly professes his homosexuality. After the ordination, the churches in the local Baptist association to which the church belongs on its Baptist side begin to circulate a petition calling for the removal of the hand of fellowship from that church. The church is stunned by this action; as a local Baptist church they had done, in their estimation, nothing wrong. The ordination and all of its proceedings and actions was in the hand of what would amount to the

[1] We note that this scenario overlaps scenarios 9 and 10 of the chapter on Soul Freedom.

local United Church of Christ. The members of the association circulating the petition were undaunted by this argument; they were guilty by association. They never should have allowed the issue to move forward, and when it did, they should have removed themselves from the alliance, seeking unity with those whose interpretations of the Bible mirrored those of the Baptist association.

Discussion Questions for Scenario 3, Part 1

1. Does a local church have freedom to set its own standards for ordination?
2. If there are qualifying restrictions, who would determine what they might be? What are the Soul Freedom implications here? What are the Biblical Authority issues here?
3. Is it possible that a gay or lesbian individual might meet the local church standards for ordination? What do we mean when we say that the answer to this question lies in the church's interpretation of Soul Freedom versus Biblical Authority?
4. What are the implications of a yoked church that is bound to two different national denominational entities, each with different standards for ordination? Is one part of the church (Baptist) bound to the polity of the other part of the church (UCC)? Should the UCC part of the church be bound, or at least sympathetic, to the polity standards of the other half of its fellowship (Baptist)? Would it make a difference if the local Baptist church in this instance were in agreement with the local UCC church?
5. What are the principles that bind individual Baptist churches together in associations?
6. Are theological or Biblical dogmatism among them? Can theological or Biblical dogmatism be one of them?
7. What would be legitimate cause for an association to remove the hand of fellowship from one of its participating churches?
8. When a church is disfellowshiped from an association, does it have a hierarchy to adjudicate the decision?
9. Where might the local church appeal the decision of the association?

10. Are the principles that bind individual believers together into a local church different from the principles that bind individual churches into an association? If yes, explain what those principles are and how they are carried out. If no, explain the differences and why those differences exist.
11. Is it possible that the local church or the local association could be guilty of selectivity in its condemnation of what is acceptable behavior within the fellowship? What do you think is being asked in this question? Why would homosexuality be chosen as a dividing issue while other "deadly sins" considered by the Scripture to be "equal" to homosexuality, such as greed, gluttony, or pride, are not considered divisive?

Part Two: The local Baptist Association did eventually vote to remove the hand of fellowship from the Baptist church in question, arguing that they could not be in fellowship with a church complicit in such an event they deemed biblically wrong. Under the standards of the American Baptist Churches, USA, the disfellowshipped church had two years to join another association. The executive director of a local region that was contiguous to the disfellowshipping region initiated dialogue, inviting the church to join its association. That started several months of very painful discussion within the inviting association, and it became quickly evident that many of the association ministers and churches did not share the view of their executive. The arguments landed on traditional sides, an open interpretation of Scripture versus a more legalistic view of Scripture and a holiness view of separation from that which in their eyes would be an abomination before God. In the end, the association board had a majority in favor, but fell short of a two-thirds vote necessary for welcoming a new church into the association, and the local church was told that it would have to find another region with which they could unite.

Discussion Questions for Scenario 3 Part 2

1. Where or what are the Baptist Principles in this unfolding story?
2. What do we mean by associational principles?
3. Identify what some of these associational principles might be?

4. If a local church cannot join the association in which it is located, should it be limited to an association with a contiguous boundary? If you say yes, why should there be such a limitation? If you say no, why would you allow such separation?
5. If the church is separated significantly from the association to which it belongs, would time, distance, and geography limit the very values that bring us together in fellowship and shared mission? If you answer yes, then why? What principles are involved? If you answer no, then why? What principles are involved?
6. Is it possible that associational principles can (and should) transcend geography, time, and distance?

4

Believer's Baptism

When Jesus was about thirty years old he made a decision to leave his established life in Nazareth. This meant leaving the carpentry shop where he had worked with his father and where he was making a living for himself and his family. It also meant that he left his family, his mother, his brothers and sisters. From Nazareth he would have walked to the Jordan River where his cousin John was leading somewhat of a religious revival, baptizing those coming from near and far, as Mark suggests "the whole Judean countryside and all the people of Jerusalem." (Mk 1:5)

Jesus himself was baptized by John in the Jordan River. As Baptists, we find meaning in Mark's image that Jesus "was coming up out of the water" (Mk 1:10).[1] It suggests that Jesus went down into the water and that this was a baptism by immersion.

We are not told what moved Jesus to make this life-changing move. We would assume it was some kind of an inner call, a nudge from God that the time was at hand for Jesus to begin his ministry here on earth. However, that Jesus was drawn to the waters of baptism calls out for our attention for it tells us that this was something very important to him, something essential to his mission. For Baptists, this baptismal act is at the core of our being, and from it we draw our name; it is a critical part of our identity.

The practice of baptism is one of the themes in the Bible that is more ambiguous than we want it to be. We would like Baptism to be neat, direct, and all wrapped up, but this is one area that is in dispute. Great religious traditions differ on what baptism means, on how and when it is accomplished, and on what it means to our lives. We each claim to have studied the Bible seriously and intently, and yet we emerge with different interpretations, each claiming that we have discovered biblical

---

[1] We note that the Greek word here is *anabaino* (to go down into). This is significant, and there will be more about it later in the chapter.

truth, and suggesting to the other that they have not. Can you not hear the old Baptist, speaking critically of infant baptism, "They ain't been washed. They've just been dry-cleaned"? The ambiguity of God's church on the subject, to "sprinkle" or to "dip," is a perfect example of diverse biblical interpretation, with two groups of believers studying identical texts coming to diametrically opposing viewpoints on their meaning.

There are some who will baptize a child as an infant, based on the faith of the parent, entering the child into the covenant of God's promise. They justify their belief and practice on Scripture, and quote chapter and verse. The child will later confirm, or accept, that act themselves. Others take a different view, saying that the decision to be baptized should be made by an individual at a time when he or she fully can understand the need for a relationship with God, can weigh the implications and consequences of that decision, and can express his or her personal desire to enter into such a relationship. These believers also justify their belief and practice with Scripture.

We Baptists are of this latter variety, squarely, decidedly, and passionately so. In this we stand against the Presbyterians, the Roman Catholics, the Lutherans, the Methodists, and the Orthodox. We do note here, and will say more later, that the form of baptism is not as important as the faith expressed in the decision to be baptized.

We came to believer's baptism because it seemed to the early Baptists in their study of Scripture that baptism followed the experience of faith. A person, then, had to be old enough, they had to have reached what we came to call "the age of responsibility" to have had such a faith experience. They had to be able to understand the meaning of this experience, and to have made a mature and responsible decision to act on their sense of God's movement in their lives.

The "age of responsibility" is unfortunately elusive. It is thought to be at a time when a youth is old enough to understand the difference between good and evil, to have a sense of their own frailty and sin, and to be able to make a mature decision to accept Jesus Christ as their Savior, knowing full well the meaning that is inherent in that decision. My home church in Randolph, Massachusetts, generally had a pastor's class for baptism as we entered into the seventh grade. We would realize that some would reach this point of discernment in life earlier, and some later. It is an individual decision and the church must be sensitive in its understanding as young people of different ages come forward to request baptism.

As Baptists we take heart in the story of the Ethiopian in the eighth chapter of the Book of Acts. He was sitting in his chariot and had before him the prophecy of Isaiah. Philip the Apostle came along and told him that this was all about Jesus Christ, and "he told him the good news of Jesus." The Ethiopian then came to a faith experience of Jesus Christ and asked what was to keep him from the waters of baptism. Immediately they entered the water and he was baptized (Acts 8:26–40).

The early Baptists saw the sequence as the preaching of the word, the hearing of the Word, the acceptance of the Word and the gift of God in Jesus Christ, and then and only then, baptism. When the Baptists emerged in the 1600s, they belonged to the church of the day and so had been baptized as infants. After they were baptized again, this time by their own choice, they were given the name of Anabaptist (meaning "to be rebaptized").

In our historic faith, baptism becomes the symbol, the outward manifestation, that faith in the saving grace of Jesus Christ has been experienced and accepted. It becomes the outward and visible sign of an inner and invisible change. Our affirmation, then, is in Believer's Baptism, that the individual baptized is a believer and has made such a profession of faith. It is an individual decision, not the decision of someone else.

Baptism, for Baptists, is one of two ordinances[2] that we celebrate, the second being the Lord's Supper.

The Mode of Baptism

Now, I want to take a side trip here and go beyond the discussion of the appropriate time for baptism to the question of the mode of baptism. The mode, or the form of baptism, at least to me, is not nearly as

---

[2] Baptists shy away from using the term "sacrament" to define Baptism and the Lord's Supper because "sacrament" implies to many the infusion of a magical power. We see experiencing the two more as an act of obedience to the commands of Jesus Christ. Norman Maring and Winthrop Hudson see some credibility in the use of "sacrament"; for a full discussion see Norman H. Maring and Winthrop S. Hudson, *A Baptist Manual of Polity and Practice*, rev. ed. (Valley Forge PA: Judson Press, 1991) 145–47.

important as the faith expression behind it, and I am not alone in this. I have some of the weight of Baptist history on my side. It is an interesting historical fact that the earliest Baptists baptized by sprinkling water upon the person. It was not until later that immersion became the primary mode of baptism. Evidence for this was found by W.H. Whitsitt who, in 1880, while studying early English church documents, discovered that the early Amsterdam church founded by Smyth and Helwys in 1609 practiced sprinkling as the mode of baptism until approximately 1641 when they moved to total immersion.[3]

I learned a lesson about this mode of baptism by sprinkling in December 1995. Until that time I had never baptized anyone except by immersion, and that was a very conscious and deliberate choice on my part. That year two individuals presented themselves to me, and neither had ever been baptized. Each wanted to be baptized, but they each had a very serious heart condition. We made the decision that immersion would be a threat to them because of their health, and instead we would do the baptism by sprinkling. Then in the year 2000, I had another instance when a man approaching ninety, in very frail health asked if I would baptize him. He and his wife had been attending our church, and one day he came in to see me. He told me that all of his family had been killed in flooding that took place in Indianapolis in 1916, that he had been a child and the sole survivor of his family. He did not remember any religious training or involvement over the years, and felt that it was time "to do something about it."

In the first instance I went to the individual's home where her family had gathered around her. In the second instance we met on a Saturday morning in the chapel, with his family surrounding him. In the third instance we did the baptism as a part of our Sunday morning chapel service.

Each experience was very powerful. We read the Scriptures, we prayed, then I asked the question: "Do you profess Jesus Christ to be your Savior and Lord?" As long as I live I will never forget the sincerity and the power of their response. "Yes, I do!" It was strong. It came from the depths of the heart. As I cupped water in my hand and put my hand

---

[3] James H. Slatton, *W.H. Whitsitt: The Man and the Controversy* (Macon GA: Mercer University Press, 2009).

on their head, baptizing them "in the name of the Father, Son, and Holy Spirit," the power of the Holy Spirit was there. It was an awesome experience. There were not many dry eyes such was the emotion that filled the space.

The lesson I learned is that we can make baptismal mode an icon. Much of the meaning of the ceremony is the faith and commitment brought by the individual being baptized. Though a different mode, sprinkling of an adult is still believer's baptism.[4]

All three of these individuals have now died, and I had the opportunity to do each of their funerals. What a privilege it was to share about the moment of their baptism. I knew of their commitment, and I had personally seen the power of its expression. I knew that these individuals had been embraced by God; there was no question at all in my mind that, upon their deaths, they had entered the presence of God and had been welcomed as faithful servants.

Having said all this, and having stated that the form of baptism is not as important as the faith expressed in the decision to be baptized or to have an earlier baptism confirmed, I do want to speak on why I personally feel that, when there is a choice, immersion is the preferred form. This is a personal statement of faith on my part, and is at the core of why I have stayed a Baptist by conviction all of these years. It also is a statement about why I suggest baptism by immersion if such baptism is possible. I would make four arguments as the foundation for my belief: Historical Practice, Archeological Evidence, Linguistic Analysis, and Theological Interpretation.

The first argument for immersion is from the Jewish practice of the time of Jesus. As archaeologists have uncovered buildings of this time they have found pools with steps leading down into them. These steps are often divided by a low wall so that one can enter on one side and exit on the other. We know that the Jews had a purification ritual where they would immerse themselves totally. Even today, that is a practice for

---

[4] Later in this chapter I will argue that there are powerful currents at work in immersion as symbolically we enter into the death and resurrection of Jesus Christ through entering the water physically and being brought back up out of it in new life. I have strong convictions on this symbolism; yet I am equally strong in my conviction expressed in these paragraphs about an alternative mode and its significance.

devout Jews on Holy Days such as Yom Kippur. We also know that there was a proselyte immersion that was required of a Gentile who converted to Judaism. They would be circumcised and they would be immersed. If such immersion was the Jewish practice, and as most of the early Christians were Jews, then it stands to reason that they would adopt this practice in the early Church as they did others.

The second argument for immersion is from what archaeology has uncovered from the early Church. In very early churches there are often pools ten to fifteen feet square and three to four feet deep. The mosaics surrounding them show that these pools were obviously baptisteries and that immersion was the form of baptism practiced.

The third argument for immersion is the nature of the word that was chosen to describe what has come to be known as baptism. The Greek word is *bapteo* or *baptizo*. In the context of the writings of the time, it is used to indicate the following: "to dip in or under," "to immerse," "to sink," "to drown, " or "to go under." The writers of the New Testament chose a word that, in the culture of their times and language had a clear connotation of immersion—of being placed in water and covered by water.

The fourth argument for immersion has to do with the language of going down and coming up. When Jesus was baptized he came up out of the water (the Greek word used is *anabaino*), which to me has a clear indication that he went down into the water. When the Ethiopian was baptized, he went down into the water (*katabaino*) and he came up out of the water (*anabaino*).

This idea of going down and coming up is very important in the Scripture, and, in fact, is a metaphor of the incarnation. It starts with the dream of Jacob in the Old Testament. In his dream, Jacob sees a ladder stretching from earth to heaven and angels are descending (the Greek word is *katabaino*) and ascending (*anabaino*) on the ladder.

In the Gospel of John, at the end of chapter one, the ladder is interpreted to be the Son of Man, and Jesus says that we will see angels descending and ascending (the Greek words are the same: *katabaino* and *anabaino*) on the Son. Thus, Jesus is the ladder that exists between heaven and earth. Again, the ladder as the Son of Man is a metaphor for Jesus entering into the world through incarnation.

The Apostle Paul picks up on this in his epistle to the Romans. He says that, in baptism, we enter into the life and death of Jesus Christ, of the death and resurrection of Jesus Christ. Going down (*katabaino*) and coming up (*anabaino*) out of the water touches us in the deepest part of the human spirit. We enter into the incarnate life of Jesus Christ, who came down into the world and went up out of the world. We believe that by going down into the water we enter with him into the darkness of the grave, and that by coming up out of the water we enter with him into the resurrection. It is the symbol of dying to sin and giving ourselves to new life. It is the symbol of the old and the new. It is the symbol of putting aside the old and becoming a new creation in Christ Jesus.

We were created by God with a complexity that is astounding. There are spiritual depths to us that, in the course of a lifetime, we just begin to fathom. We know that we are touched deeply by symbols and by meaning, and it is my belief that God has created the baptism experience to touch us at the deepest part of our lives as we enter into it. It touches us beyond our capacity to understand, but we do have a glimpse that it is both deep and profound. To join with Jesus in death and resurrection is our call to faith; to participate with Jesus in the act of baptism brings a relationship beyond any power I have of description.

Baptism begins a lifelong journey of immersing ourselves in the life, the death, and the ministry of Jesus Christ. It moves us profoundly as we approach it, seeking the mind and heart of Jesus Christ.

For many of us who were baptized at a young age, the meaning of baptism is a process that grows in and upon us. We were young and naïve at the time, and yet we were at the age of responsibility and we did understand something. It was the beginning of our journey and a milestone in our lives, but we will spend all of our lives growing into the potential for what it can mean.

We are called to faith and baptism by the gospel. I have made the point that both immersion and sprinkling have a place. Yet I am convicted that immersion most fully embodies the full Scriptural meaning. We as Baptists acknowledge that neither baptism nor the form of baptism is essential for salvation. We also affirm that we personally believe that immersion is the biblical mode, bringing incredible layers of meaning to the journey that we walk each day.[5]

Open Membership

I would be remiss if I did not address the matter of open membership in Baptist churches. What does a church do when a potential new member seeks membership and discovers that they have not been baptized by immersion? Many churches have an associate membership, and bring the individual in as a partial member who is not able to fully participate in the life and ministry of the church. In some instances, these individuals are restricted from the Lord's Table. In other instances, they are restricted from voting in church meetings. Sometimes they are restricted only on voting on the call of a new minister, or certain budget details. Many of these churches are in the South, and this is one way they could involve the "snowbirds"—those who flocked to warmer regions during the cold, northern months.

Other churches practice open membership. They will accept new members into full church membership even though they have not been baptized by immersion. Some require that the individual be baptized in some form, usually sprinkling from one of the churches that practice that form of baptism, but others will accept new members without any baptism at all.

As I have read literature and periodicals on this subject in recent years, it seems to be a relatively "hot" issue, for there has been a lot of discussion. It has been of particular interest that several writers have buttressed their argument with quotes from early Anabaptists and Baptists, making the point that this open membership idea is not something new, it has been rolling around the Church for quite some time.

---

[5] Resources for this chapter included: George Tooze, *Reflections on Baptism,* sermons preached 27 November 1983 and 13 February 1994; Gerhard Kittel, ed., *Theological Dictionary of the New Testament,* vol. 1, trans. Geoffrey W. Bromiley, 529–46; Norman H. Maring and Winthrop S. Hudson, *A Baptist Manual of Polity and Practice* (Valley Forge PA: Judson Press, 1963); O.C.S. Wallace, *What Baptists Believe,* The Sunday School Board of the Southern Baptist Convention, 1934; Alexander Carson, *Baptism in its Mode and Subjects* (Philadelphia: American Baptist Publication Society, 1860).

Baptists Today in its December 2009 issue published a letter from an older Baptist who lamented the lack of standards in the more "modern" Baptist churches, one of them being open membership, that is, not requiring baptism by immersion. William Hardee provided a very thoughtful answer, pointing out that, as early as 1673, John Bunyan of *Pilgrim's Progress* fame had "warned of making an idol of God's ordinance of water baptism."[6] He also quoted G. Todd Wilson, saying: "open church membership has existed from our earliest beginnings."[7]

In the same issue of *Baptists Today*, Curtis Freeman also had an article on the subject. He observed that, "Daniel Turner, an 18th century English Baptist Minister, argued that by excluding any of God's children from the means of grace, 'we are guilty of invading the prerogative of Christ.'"[8] In other words, if Jesus Christ will accept individuals without baptism by immersion, why can't his Church?

I know that someone is going to ask me about my own belief and experience regarding open membership. It is a fair question. In my Indianapolis congregation we did practice open membership, though it was open membership in the form of my asking that new members have experienced some kind of baptism before they joined our church. If they had had a prior baptismal experience of sprinkling, that was acceptable. If they had never been baptized in any form, then I asked them to either be immersed or sprinkled. I felt that it was important that we follow the example of Jesus. With those who had been baptized as infants and confirmed, I explained to them the meaning of believer's baptism and the powerful experience and symbolism that were to be found in immersion. Some chose to stay with what they had; others requested that they be immersed. Interestingly, over the years, there were a number who chose to come in with their infant baptism, who later, after growing in their life of faith and seeing others being immersed, would change their mind and ask for immersion for themselves. I bear testimony that for a pastor, there

[6] William L. Hardee, "Open letter, open response to questions about being Baptist," *Baptists Today* (December 2009): 14–16.

[7] G. Todd Wilson, "Why Baptists Should Not Rebaptize Christians from Other Denominations," in *Proclaiming the Baptist Vision: Baptism and the Lord's Supper*, ed. Walter B. Shurden (Macon GA: Smyth & Helwys, 1999) 41–49.

[8] Curtis W. Freedom, "Baptists and baptism at year 400," *Baptists Today* (December 2009): 17.

is no more powerful experience than baptizing a person who has had a transformative faith experience, and who asks for baptism out of that experience.

Topics for Discussion

Baptism Scenario 1

The parents of a young six year old pull you aside after church and tell you that their daughter has asked them if she could be baptized. You explain to them about the Baptist version of the "age of accountability" and suggest that historically six years old has been on the younger side of what most Baptist churches allow for baptism. You talk to them about the seriousness of making a decision to accept Jesus Christ as Savior and Lord and following him in the waters of baptism. All the while you are saying these things they are nodding their heads and finally as you finish your explanation they smile broadly and exclaim that they are absolutely sure that their six year old understands all of these things. She is mature for her age they tell you, and they really believe that she is ready for baptism.

Discussion Questions for Scenario 1

1. What are your initial thoughts?
2. Would it make a difference if the child were 9 years? 11 years old?
3. Is there a culture in some families and churches that, for whatever reason, it is important that their children "get saved," with baptism being a symbol of this?
4. Is it possible that this could be such an instance?
5. Listening to your intuition, do you think that this is a decision that the young girl has made, or a decision that her parents have made?
6. Does it matter that the parents are asking rather than the child?
7. What decision to their request are you formulating in your mind?
8. What do you think are, within the life of your local church, the congregational ramifications of such a decision?

9. What would be the ramifications if you agreed to the baptism? What would be the ramifications if you did not agree to the baptism?
10. Is baptism or church membership a decision that the pastor can make, or is there another body involved such as the deacons, diaconate, governing board, or council?
11. What is the process for membership in your church?
12. How would you go about making that decision? Would you talk to the six-year-old child and try to discern for yourself? Would you take the word of her parents?
13. What would be the wisdom in counseling a waiting period of another year? Several years? What would have to change? What more than the passage of time would you need to see and hear that you are not seeing and hearing now?
14. What else do you say to them?
15. What are the questions you ask? What are the statements you make?
16. What is your final action?

Commentary on Scenario 1

In my Indianapolis congregation, a very cumbersome membership process was in place when I arrived in 1983. An individual would come forward and ask for baptism and/or membership; they would then meet with representatives from the deacons. That report would go to the pastor, and then it would go to the Membership Commission. On the vote of the Membership Commission it would go to the Administrative Council. Only when that vote was taken could the hand of fellowship be offered; unfortunately it was a process that could take a couple of months.

As we looked at reorganization, it was observed that when most individuals presented themselves for membership they were already known to the pastoral staff, for they had been active for some time and often pastoral staff had met with them. The staff knew their backgrounds, their church relationship, and their baptismal status; with this, the pastoral staff were authorized to give the hand of fellowship to individuals upon their presentation if such circumstances were known. If baptism was requested, or if the individual was new and the information was unavailable, the hand of fellowship was not extended until such process was given.

For the most part the membership decisions were left in pastoral hands.

Baptism Scenario 2

A young family begins to attend your church because the mother has become the paid section leader (soprano) in your choir. They finally decide that they would like to join the church. You explain to them that baptism by immersion is required for membership, and the father of the family explains to you that he grew up in a Lutheran home, that his father is a Lutheran minister active in a local church in the Indianapolis community. He explains that his father baptized him as a baby, and he confirmed that baptism as a young man. He said that this whole process was one of life's significant experiences for him and for his family, and he felt that his whole experience would be cheapened if he were forced to go through another form of baptism simply to fulfill a membership requirement. You are sympathetic but also bound by the bylaws of your church.

Discussion Questions for Scenario 2

1. What are your initial thoughts?
2. Do you think this individual is principled or just plain stubborn?
3. Is it possible in the life of a church for the act of baptism by immersion to become an idol? What do you think is meant by the question above?
4. What do you think would be accomplished by insisting that this baptism take place?
5. Do you think the individual would experience "real" salvation? Is baptism necessary for salvation or just that the bylaws be fulfilled? What would happen if you asked the church to waive the bylaws in this instance?
6. Do you think the man and his family would be glad that the church insisted on his immersion?
7. What are the implications when a pastor's conscience conflicts with the official bylaws of the church?

8. What is the meaning of open membership and is it helpful in this situation?
9. Do you see a creative way out of this dilemma?
10. What would you propose doing?

Commentary on Scenario 2

This is an actual situation which took place at First Baptist Church in Indianapolis many, many years ago. The man in the story is still an active member of that church; it would not be wrong to say that, over the years, he has played a very significant leadership role in the life of the congregation. He did go ahead with the baptism, in part to meet the legalistic requirement of the church for membership, though also out of some respect for the history and beliefs of the church. The situation did in fact cause some difficulty with his father and his extended family, though, as families do, they were eventually able to work through the issues that had emerged. I came to the church a number of years after this incident, and by that time the by-laws had been changed to say that the pastor, for sufficient reason, had the authority to waive baptism by immersion.

Baptism Scenario 3

An individual approaches you and asks if you would consider allowing her to be rebaptized. She relates how she had been immersed at a younger age and, looking back, she does not feel that she had sufficient understanding; now with a stronger faith she would like to bear testimony to her spiritual growth through rebaptism. In talking with her you doubt neither her strong interest nor her sincerity in asking.

You explain to her the very nature of the faith journey. For most of us it is a series of failures and successes, falling down and rising up, sin and redemption. At each stage we are stronger because we have learned and grown in our understanding so that with age we might even reach some maturity in our life of faith. If we wanted to be rebaptized at significant growth points in our lives to reaffirm our faith, then there is the possibility that we could have an infinite number of rebaptisms—at which point baptism becomes more robotic and functional, if not narcissistic, than holy and spiritual. Our original baptism grows with us as we grow and appreciate its hidden dimensions and the firm foundation it gives us on our faith journey.

When you finish, she tells you that she does appreciate your thought, and your warning about the dangers of rebaptism, but she would like to go ahead with it anyway, if you are willing.

Discussion Questions for Scenario 3

1. What are your initial thoughts as you read this?
2. Would you personally ever ask for rebaptism?
3. If you would ask for rebaptism, what would be the circumstances that would bring you to do that?
4. What would you say to make a compelling case to allow rebaptism?
5. What would you say to make a compelling case to deny rebaptism?
6. After reading the commentary below, what do you think about the "only once" rule? Do you think the arguments for the "only once" rule are adequate to make a case?
7. What would be meant with the statement that after a number of rebaptisms the issue could become psychological as opposed to spiritual?

Commentary on Scenario 3

The request for rebaptism occurs far more often than one would think. I was surprised at the number of times it came up. When it did, I took each case individually and would spend time talking to the person, trying to get a sense as to where they were spiritually, and what might be going on in their lives that would call for such an action. I can't remember that I ever turned someone down, for in the end I felt that I had to trust and to believe their soul competency and their faith quest. I did tell them that I personally would only rebaptize them once, that to go further than that would make me think the issue might be more psychological than spiritual, and that was a rule from which I did not deviate.

Baptism Scenario 4

Acts 10 tells the story of Cornelius and Peter. Cornelius is a Roman Centurion who practiced both Jewish piety and generosity. He receives a vision that he is to send to Joppa for Peter, asking Peter to return for a visit to the home of Cornelius. Meanwhile Peter has a vision from God as to what is clean and unclean, the meaning of which is that God is about to break down some of the traditional barriers. "What God has made clean, you must not call profane" (Acts 10:15). Then he has another vision that he is to go with the men sent by Cornelius.

To make a long story short, Peter overcomes his aversion that Cornelius is a Gentile. He obeys by going to the home of Cornelius and proclaims the gospel to Cornelius and his family. As Peter is speaking, the Holy Spirit falls upon them all and those circumcised with Peter are absolutely astounded that the Holy Spirit would fall upon these heathen uncircumcised Gentiles. But the work of the Holy Spirit is obvious, and Peter comes to the conclusion that no one can "withhold the water for baptizing these people who have received the Holy Spirit just as we have" (Acts 10:47).

When Peter returns to Jerusalem, the other apostles and the "circumcised believers" become very critical of Peter; that he would even eat with these people, never mind agreeing to baptize them into the faith, is an abomination. Peter tells the story and ends with his powerful and wonderful conclusion, "If God gave them the same gift that he gave us when we believed in the Lord Jesus Christ, who was I that I could hinder God?" (Acts 11:17). With that they are silenced, though shortly they too are able to say, "Then God has given even to the Gentiles the repentance that leads to life." (Acts 11:18)

Discussion Questions for Scenario 4

1. What are your initial thoughts as you read this?
2. Is it possible, thinking about open membership within the Baptist church, that requiring baptism by immersion for membership in every instance is very much the same kind of idol that circumcision was to the early Church?
3. If this is true, is it possible that the church could be told, as was the early Jerusalem Council, to move beyond idolatry?

4. Is it possible that God might move beyond requirements, looking instead for evidence of the Holy Spirit at work in the life of an individual? If we claim the power of God through the Holy Spirit to be at work in us, and we do not move forward for baptism and church membership, do we deny or denigrate that work of God?
5. If we say that baptism is such a powerful experience for the believer (and we all agree that it should be and that it is), in requiring it for membership are we making our own experience the norm? Or are we making our history the norm? Or are we making our convictions the norm? Or are we making our soul competency the norm?
6. Does the Bible *teach* us that a believer should want to follow Jesus in the waters of baptism, that we follow in his footsteps (i.e. be baptized)?
7. Does the Bible *require* us to follow Jesus in the waters of baptism that we might do what he did (i.e. be baptized)?
8. Do you think in asking these questions that I've moved from preaching to meddling?

Baptism Scenario 5

It is the first time that you have ever participated in the ordinance of baptism. You enter into the baptismal pool, you read the liturgy appropriate for the occasion, you turn and you motion the first candidate for baptism to enter the water with you. You ask him if he has accepted Jesus Christ as Savior and Lord, and with his affirmation you say: "Upon your profession of faith, and in obedience to Jesus Christ, I bury you with him in baptism, that you might rise with him in newness of life." After you have placed him under the water, to your great distress, you note as you bring him back up, that the top of his head is still dry. You did not get him completely under the water.

Discussion Questions for Scenario 5

1. I suspect that you are laughing! But what are you thinking?
2. Do you think nothing of it, congratulate him, and send him out of the pool?
3. Are you are horrified that you have made a terrible mistake?

4. Do you think that while he has not been completely immersed, he certainly is a step up from having been sprinkled?
5. Do you fear the implications of his going through life, unknowingly having had an incomplete baptism by immersion experience, and would it be your fault?
6. What do *you* think are the implications of an incomplete act of immersion?
7. Would you explain to him later what had happened and suggest that he might want to be rebaptized?
8. Would you say that anything worth doing is worth doing right and rebaptize him right then and there?

Commentary for Scenario 5

When I attended seminary, Nelson Elliott, who taught the Baptist Polity Class, had a day during the semester when he took the students over to a baptistery in a local Baptist church, and had them practice baptism on each other as a learning experience. His wife Priscilla used to laugh and say that with Nelson's practicing, she had been immersed more times than anyone else in the world. His intention was a lesson on how to baptize someone competently and gracefully so that once in a pastorate one could approach the situation with confidence. Unfortunately for me, I was home ill in bed the day that the class had practice on immersion techniques.

In my first year as associate minister at the First Baptist Church of Beverly, we had a number of candidates to baptize during the Easter season. As was the custom, I was to take half of them and John Wilbur, the senior minister, would baptize the other half. For whatever reason, I ended up with the first group, and a young man named L(enny) A(uld) (it was the tradition to go alphabetically) was the first candidate.

Yes, as he came up out of the water, I noted the dryness of the top of his head. I realized later that I didn't even think about it. I'm not sure there was a rational process. It was an intuitive, immediate response as I immediately, without saying a word to him or to anyone else, put him back down into the water again.

To say that he was surprised would be an understatement. But he never asked me about it nor did anyone in the congregation that evening. Nor did I ever say anything about it to him and I cannot remember talking about it with anyone else. I suspect that somewhere, someplace, there was a discussion on why the Reverend Tooze double-dipped one of his candidates. Did they miss something? Was he breaking new ground? Was there some hidden symbolic meaning here?

I can assure you of one thing. In the forty years of ministry that followed, there was never another who came up dry.

Baptism Scenario 6

This story was told to me by one of the members of my church as we shared in an early morning Bible Study group. She had received a telephone call that her brother was near death and in the hospital's critical care unit. She went to see him, thinking as she went that she had two concerns. The first was for his health; the second was for his spiritual state, for he had never been active in a church and had never, to her knowledge, made a profession of faith. When she arrived, he was tethered to machines and could not verbally respond to her in any way; she did notice that his eyes were clear and responsive, and as she talked he would respond to her in that way. She spoke to him of her faith, about God's great love that came to us in Jesus Christ, and when she asked him if he wanted to respond to God's great invitation he indicated that he did. "I began to weep," she said "and then I thought to myself that I wanted to baptize him. I looked around and did not see any water readily available." With this she paused, looking around at the group; she had the rapt attention of everyone at that table. And then quietly she said, "So I baptized him with my tears."

Discussion Questions for Scenario 6

1. What are your initial thoughts as you read this story?
2. What would you have done in such a situation?
3. At that moment, in that situation, was baptism necessary? Was this a legitimate baptism? Can a layperson baptize a new person in the faith?
4. Is there any such thing as "insufficient water" in performing a baptism? In other words, would a teardrop be sufficient?
5. Does the situation as told waive some of the rules? Necessarily so?

6. Is it possible that the church sometimes has more stringent rules than God does?

Commentary on Scenario 6

Ginger Hoyt is a member of First Baptist Church, Indianapolis, and part of an early Wednesday morning Bible Study Group that I led. She told this story and later wrote it out for me to relate here. In the story she told of her only brother, who differed with her in religious beliefs, but who also loved to have long dialogues with her on religion. They differed on what was meant by being "saved by faith," and he differed on any future hope in eternity.

On the day that he died she visited with him in the intensive care unit of the hospital; he seemed to be unresponsive, she knew this would be the last time she would see him.

She spoke to him of matters of faith. "I sensed that he was aware of that now. I asked if he was at last convinced that God was real and that Jesus had come to convince us of that fact. He seemed to respond and I strongly sensed [his affirmation]. Then, just out of the blue I asked if he would like to be baptized in Jesus' name and accept and acknowledge Christ as Savior. Yes again!"

A thousand thoughts processed through her mind. What to do? Then the thought came that she was a Certified Lay Minister, and "[I] thanked the Lord that if all of that study and work in addition to working full time and family and volunteering was just to prepare for this one moment, it was worth it."

She asked herself what to use for water, and could he stand the shock. Then the answer came:

> You have plenty of water, it is dripping abundantly down your face. Use your tears!
>
> Thus with my tears and in the name of God the Father, Jesus the Christ the savior and son, and through the promised power of the Holy Spirit, I dipped my finger in my tears and made a cross on my dear dying brother's forehead and consecrated his soul for eternity.
>
> Was it real? Yes, for me and for my brother it was completely real. Did he die? Yes, he died within a few hours after I left the hospital for home. Was Skip saved? Yes, I believe he was and we will discuss it someday.

> We spend our lives preparing for instances that take moments of our time. Life is not so much about how much we prepare ourselves as it is about the choices we make and how we act on those choices. I have learned that big blessings are usually very painful but not to be avoided and even cowards like me have the courage to participate in them. Through the power of faith.[9]

Baptism Scenario 7

In the announcements made during your Sunday morning worship service, the pastor announces that several weeks hence there will be a service of Believer's Baptism by immersion, and the pastor invites any who might wish to be involved in that service to speak to a member of the Diaconate at the close of the service. He/she then says a word about the Baptist profession of faith and the course that we believe that faith and baptism should take:

First there is the proclamation of the biblical Word, calling for faith in Jesus Christ as savior and Lord;

Secondly there is the acceptance of Jesus Christ as savior and Lord by the individual person, in which they enter into a personal relationship with him;

Thirdly there is baptism by immersion, an outward and visible sign of an inward and invisible experience in which the individual, through baptism, enters into the death and resurrection of Jesus Christ;

Finally, following baptism, the individual is welcomed into the body of Christ, the church.

Part One: Following the Sunday worship service, one of the new people in church approaches a member of the diaconate for the first time and states that he would like to participate in the Service of Baptism. They ask him if he can comfortably make a profession of faith in Jesus Christ as his Lord and Savior. He respond that yes, he can indeed. Then the conversation between the two of them goes something like this:

Diaconate Member: "Praise the Lord. What great news this is. I'll be in touch with you sometime this week and we'll get things rolling."

---

[9] This story was taken from a document prepared for me by Ginger Hoyt, Indianapolis, Indiana.

Candidate: "Thank you. I'll look forward to that!"

Diaconate Member: "I'll also send you the paperwork and have you fill it out, so that we can get the information we need for our records as you join our church."

Candidate: "Do I have to join the church?"

Diaconate Member: "Well, Baptism and church membership usually goes hand in hand."

Candidate: "Do I have to join the church?"

Diaconate Member: "Well—yes! (Pause) Well—no! (Pause) Well—I've never asked or answered that question before because I've never had to. Well—I'll have to do some thinking about that? Tell me—why don't you want to join the church?

Candidate: "I guess I'm just not ready. But I know that I am ready to be baptized.

Discussion Questions for Scenario 7, Part 1

1. What are your initial thoughts as you read this?
2. What do you think are the Baptist Principles at work here?
3. Do baptism and church membership go hand in hand? If they do, should they?
4. What do you think is the meaning of church membership?
5. Can a person be a believer and not be an active member of the church? Can a person be an active member of the church and not be a believer?
6. What is the advantage to joining the church as opposed to simply attending? (Maybe they are aware of the bylaw requirement that non-members cannot serve on church committees!)
7. Where does such a decision lie?
8. Does she/he make a decision?
9. Does she/he bring it to a pastor or one of the governing boards—deacons, diaconate, governing board, council—of the church?
10. What would you say to this individual?
11. Would you go ahead with their baptism?

Part Two: Following the worship service, the second person to speak to you is an elderly man. He and his wife had been attending the church for quite some time, and his wife had recently died. He tells you that he was orphaned at an early age, and that his family of origin was Roman Catholic. The recent death of his wife had got him thinking; he cannot remember any baptism experience, or any confirmation experience. He says that he does not have any record of being baptized and there are no pictures of such an event or experience in extended family photo albums. He would like to have that experience of his faith; however he believes it questionable that, at his age, he could participate in a service of immersion.[10]

Discussion Questions for Scenario 7, Part 2

1. What are your initial thoughts?
2. Would you simply tell him of God's great love and that his lack of baptism would not have any consequences before God?
3. Would you tell him that you would plan to immerse him, knowing that you would be very gentle in doing the baptism?
4. Is it possible for a Baptist preacher to baptize an individual in any form other than immersion?
5. If yes to the above, what might those circumstances be? If so, what might be the mode? If so, what might be the requirements?
6. Is baptism by immersion a requirement for salvation? If it is not, why do you think there would be some churches that would continue to insist on it?
7. What, if any, are the implications of a non-immersion baptism in the life (politics) of the church?
8. Would you personally be comfortable baptizing someone by sprinkling?
9. Would it change your thinking on baptism by sprinkling if the person had no physical limitation that would require sprinkling; they just simply wanted to do it the "easier" way?

Part Three: Following the worship service, a couple speaks to you. They have been attending for some time, and they would like to join the

[10] This story is found as well in this chapter under "Mode of Baptism."

church. They would be transferring their membership from the Baptist church they had been attending in the community in which they formerly lived. In talking to them you realize that the husband had grown up in a Baptist church, and had been immersed with a profession of faith when he was a young teen. The wife, however, had grown up in another tradition; she had been sprinkled, had confirmed that baptism, and because the last Baptist church to which they belonged practiced open membership, they did not require her to be immersed in order to join. Thus you realize that you would be taking into membership someone who had not been immersed, and while you might be willing to make an exception for health or physical ailment reasons, she was and is perfectly healthy and would be well able to experience immersion. Your church is one that does require immersion for membership, unless the requirement is waived for a compelling reason.

Discussion Questions for Scenario 7, Part 3

1. What are your first thoughts as you think about this?
2. Do you laugh at "the tangled webs" we weave for ourselves?
3. Does your church require baptism by immersion? What is in the bylaws?
4. If baptism is required, do the bylaws allow any exceptions?
5. Do you think that you as a minister or church leader should require baptism by immersion?
6. Would you like to officially have some wiggle room?
7. Does your church give you, as the pastor or one of the lay leaders, the right to make allowances for different situations that might test or bend the rules?
8. Are her reasons for not being immersed compelling?
9. Irrespective of the baptism issue, does your church simply allow a clear straightforward transfer from another Baptist church?
10. Would you say that this scenario illustrates one of the dangers of allowing open membership?
11. Does this mean that in the future, you are going to have to check every transfer and make sure it is not from an open membership church and that the individual is not "coming into the kingdom through the back door?"

Part Four: Following the worship service, the fourth person to speak to you (you're having a long day at the door) is an individual who would like to join your church. He thanks you for talking about baptism, but he tells you that he feels no need for it. His faith, his acceptance of Jesus Christ, his desire to belong and serve, is sufficient. While you might be willing to accept a person who has experienced a different form of Baptism—after all they have been baptized—you wonder if perhaps this is pushing a little beyond your tolerance limits.

Discussion Questions for Scenario 7, Part 4

1. What are your initial thoughts as you read this?
2. Does a person need to experience baptism before joining the church?
3. Allowing a "yes"—would you stipulate that it need only be baptism in some form? Or would you stipulate solely immersion? Or would you open the door wide no matter what?
4. Suppose that Jesus were standing at the door with you, what would he be whispering in your ear? What would the church administrative body be whispering in your ear?
5. Is it possible that the administrative body and Jesus might be whispering contradictory messages?
6. Do you think you might lose him/her if you didn't take them in as a member?
7. Would you care if you lost him/her—at least you would avoid "the problem" he/she represents.
8. Would you treat him/her differently if he/she was a company president, wealthy, and a tither?

5

Biblical Authority

Good preaching has a way of rubbing people the wrong way, especially if it crosses the lines of culture and tradition. In the eleventh chapter of Mark's gospel we read of Jesus preaching, first by deed, and then by word. The chapter opens with the triumphal entry into Jerusalem and the cleansing of the temple, followed the next day by the disciples seeing the withered fig tree and Jesus teaching the disciples on prayer. Through all of this there are very clear statements of who Jesus understands himself to be (his messianic declaration), of the responsibilities that come with this understanding (rooting out the corruption and injustice of the religious system embodied in the temple), and of what it means to live together in community (do not pray for forgiveness for yourself if there is someone whom you have not forgiven).

The chief priests, the scribes, and the elders who have been "rubbed" the wrong way are waiting for Jesus as soon as he enters the temple, and they get right to the heart of the matter. "By what authority are you doing these things? Who gave you this authority to do them?" (Mk 11:48). They are asking Jesus who he is, who gave him the right to do and say what he was doing and saying, and why would it be binding on their lives. We must not let the apparent simplicity of the questions distract us from their hostility. The questions are deadly serious, as are the priests, scribes, and elders, who, within days, will convince Pontius Pilate to execute Jesus.

The Jewish leaders lived by their own authority, which was grounded in the covenant with Abraham. God had called them, then reinforced that calling and authority through Moses, who had been led by God to bring them out of Egypt. God had been with the Jews in the wilderness for forty years, finally bringing them into the Promised Land. He had made them a great nation under David. Through the prophets, continued revelation from God had been proclaimed to the Jews, despite exile and subordination by numerous foreign invaders. With this history of God's faithfulness, the Jews had a culture of law and practice, of sacrifice; it was authority buttressed by God's Word (what today we would know as the Old Testament) and by tradition (the Law as it had unfolded in interpretative practice). It was the responsibility of the Jews to preserve this authority, and thus to be careful with, and judgmental of, Jesus the interloper, who was disrupting all that they had been given and all that they valued as truth with his questions, his teaching, and his deeds.[1]

The question of authority is still relevant for us today. "By what authority are you doing these things? Who gave you this authority to do them?" (Mk 11:28). It is a question for the Church, for those engaged in or thinking about engaging in pastoral ministry, and for individual Christians struggling to find their place and ministry within the world. What motivates us? What is the source of our truth? Why do we do what we do? What are the foundational beliefs that are the rock upon which we stand?

It is our belief as the Church and as individual Christians that our authority is God, who speaks to us through Scripture interpreted by the power of the Holy Spirit.

Authority Alternatives

For our purposes, I will look at five different possibilities as we review authoritative sources. Four of them I believe are pretenders; I will classify them as the oral tradition (teaching), the practical tradition (historical practice), the creeds and councils (historic decisions), personal

[1] Over my ministerial career I have approached this challenge of Jesus by the Jewish leaders from a number of different viewpoints. Certainly there is reason to suspect that the leaders were trying to protect the status quo and their status, power, or position that the status quo allowed them to have. Certainly it is fair to say that their religious faith had been institutionalized and that it would be very difficult for them to look at it in an entirely new way as Jesus was asking them to do. More recently I have come to believe that misguided or whatever, they sincerely believed in the traditions of their faith. Thus believing, they saw Jesus as someone to be defended against. Instead of seeing him as a breath of fresh air, a new revelation, a fuller understanding, they saw him as a threat to centuries of their way of life.

experience (the inner voice and discernment). The last is absolute and real; it is Scripture alone (*Sola Scriptura*).

Books have been written on each of these areas, but this is not my intent. It is my purpose here simply to identify these alternatives and a few of the problems they present, not to definitively argue their pros and cons. I will move deeper into our convictions around *Sola Scriptura*.

Oral Tradition

The oral tradition embodies centuries of the spoken word taught and preached, so it is not just a word or a thought, an idea or an expression, but rather a continuous line (unbroken we would have to assume) that contains the cumulative weight of time and history. It reflects the apostles, the church fathers, and the history of church leadership. Because oral tradition is dependent upon memory and tempered by circumstance, we have to assume some kind of continuity of thought and practice filtered through the testing experiences of the ages. Truth might be validated by the weight of history lived out in real life.

Over the centuries much of the oral tradition has been transcribed and published, so we have vast amounts of information available to us. We have published sermons, as well as reflections of hermits sequestered in the desert; we have printed theological treatises that were pivotal at crucial, transitional times in the life of the Church. Much of our tradition was inspired—certainly ancient Church leaders were not deprived of the inspiration and guidance of the Holy Spirit. One such example is Tertullian's famous line, "the blood of the martyrs is the seed of the Church." This is believed to be true.

The Scripture has informed all of this oral tradition in written form, with most of it being interpretative of that Scripture. This, however, makes the oral tradition secondary to Scripture, makes it dependent upon Scripture, and thus, in my opinion, makes it a secondary resource, unable to meet the criteria for being either Scripture or authoritative.

Practical Tradition

Traditions evolve from primary events. Something is experienced and has great meaning, so the experience is repeated with the same meaningful results anticipated. The passage of years brings a kind of sacredness to this reoccurring event, for so much of our individual being is nurtured by it. It has great power in our life; we look forward to it with anticipation; we experience it with pleasure; we draw from it a sense of well-being, and already we begin to look hopefully to the next time we are to be involved in it.

Traditions evolve in our life experiences, in our families, in our cities and nations, and in our churches. They can have a life span of several years, a decade, a quarter century, a century or several, and even multiple centuries.

We know that many of our rituals endure because they are rooted deeply in the human quest for God. They are time-honored to achieve what they were intended to achieve, helping us to live peacefully with one another, helpful in maintaining our relationship with God.

As I sit in worship I am lifted by the towering arches of the church we attend, with the sun lighting up the stained glass windows and throwing layers of sparkling colors to my imagination. I am enthralled by the power of the organ in the prelude and postlude, and lifted when the organist interpolates the hymn into soaring rhythms that touch me deeply. I am transfixed by the power of excellent preaching that nags at my conscience and lifts me to higher possibilities. I am challenged when the gospel lesson overlaps with the Old Testament reading, and then if the epistle texts add another dimension, it is a feast for my mind and heart. These traditions have endured for a long time, and I am touched by them. I find great meaning in them.

They can easily become rote, however, without recognition of their roots. In one family the daughter was taught that when she cooked the Easter ham, she was to cut a slice off each end before cooking it, a task she did dutifully for many years. One year she asked her mother about the origin of the tradition, and the mother had to think for a moment. Then with a laugh she said, "When your father and I were first married, our oven was too small for a whole ham, so I cut a slice off each end."

Practical traditions are embodied in the phrase "but we've always done it this way," suggesting that time, history, and repetition make for compelling truth. We know, however, that this is simply not true. Individuals change; cultures changes. Our needs differ over the years. We grow in understanding and seek what is deeper and more satisfying. I spoke above about my feelings for the traditions of worship; as I write I realize that the traditions are changing and that many do not feel the same way I do; they are not moved by, nor inspired by, the same things that move and inspire me. They are content with a building as opposed to a soaring sanctuary; they prefer electronic music to the organ, praise music to gospel hymns. They prefer conversation to oratory. This is neither right nor wrong; it is simply different, and we find that traditions can be frail and yet in tension. One new minister changed the order of worship, and was confronted by an elderly matron who reminded him that "you may have gone to Harvard and Yale sonny, but in this church we always take the offering after the sermon!"

The difficulty comes with discerning the roots of the practice. We understand how much of what we do is rooted in the politics of an organization, or the culture, or specific events that were a challenge to the Church at one time, and the ritual came out of meeting that need. These rituals may have enduring qualities, but they are interpretative, not original. They came out of Scripture or worship or celebration, which means that they are secondary as opposed to primary, and thus do not meet the criteria for being Scripture or authoritative.

Creeds and Councils

Creeds, confessions of faith,[2] the documents produced by the earliest leaders and thinkers within the life of the Church certainly have authority within them. They came, in most instances, from councils called by the wider Church leadership to dialogue around theological questions, biblical interpretation, functions within the life of the Church itself.

Many of them are specific for a time, intending to counter certain practices or thoughts deemed to be heretical by Church leaders. They came out of theological trends, interpretative biblical application, and practice, as the Church tried to measure what was happening as events and experiences went up against biblical truth as they understood it. The creeds, confessions, and documents were intended as a compass, giving a true direction for the journey being made by the Church at that point in time.

---

[2] We want to note that there is more on creeds and confessions of faith in the chapter on the Priesthood of the Individual Believer. Baptists generally reject creeds, calling themselves a confessional people.

We have much to learn from them. They are deeply theological, pulling together wide reaching themes into cogent statements that our minds can begin to encompass. They reflect a synthesis of thought into a meaningful declaration of faith. They summarize great truths into memorable statements that can be brought to mind when we need to remember our foundations and be inspired by them. They inform us currently in our journey of faith and discernment. Many issues are timeless and overlapping, and looking back to see how challenges were historically met can help us establish a firm foundation for ourselves in the age in which we live.

We assume that creeds, confessions of faith, and writings of the Church fathers are inspired by God, or at least we know that such is claimed. I am in mind of the old saying, "it seemed good to us and to the Holy Spirit," suggesting that any expression that came out of diligent prayer and conversation, was God-led.

Nevertheless, I would suggest that these creeds and confessions, while guided by God, are derivative. They come out of Scripture, but they are not Scripture. They are second tier to the dictates of the Scripture, trying to encapsulate the teaching of the Scripture in a contemporary setting.

Personal Experience

All of us have had a personal experience of God that has profoundly touched and changed our lives. Those of us who are Baptist believe that such personal experiences of God are the foundation for all personal faith. We speak of such experiences in terms of revelation, for they bring to us the knowledge of God's existence—God is in a personal relationship with us. These experiences drive us to learn more about God and what it means to be a follower of God.

I know that my own personal experience of God has great authority for me, for it fully defines who I am, my understanding of the love that God has for me, and the way(s) in which God has reached out to embrace me. At the same time I understand that there is a deeper authority to which the personal must bow, that of the Scripture in which the God who touched my life is revealed more completely. The Scripture informs the personal experience, though it is the personal experience that validates what we read in the pages of Scripture. It is the Scripture that tells us

God's story, and the personal experience that validates the truth of God's existence and God at work in the world. With this, the Scripture is primary, but beyond this, there are some very practical issues in making personal experience authoritative.

First there is the problem of making our own experience normative for others; God speaks to us individually in a plethora of ways, with each experience being unique, and I hesitate to say that "your" experience can be valid only if it is identical to "mine," or "my" experience can be valid only if it is identical to "yours."

Second, it is my experience that a great deal of violence comes out of people who tell us that God has spoken to them and told them to perform a particular, violent act. We realize that "psychosis" and "God speak" can sometimes be one and the same, with the results contradictory to everything we believe about how God would wish us to relate to God's creation and its population.

Third, the practice of the Church has taught that experiences of God must be validated by time and by God's people. My "call," my "experience" is only seen as reality when time shows that God is in the result and the people of God have affirmed it as being authentic.[3]

Fourth, if we are dependent on a vibrant relationship with God, we are very aware that God is sometimes silent and we are brought to what the ancients called "the dark night of the soul." In the 2007 publication of the journals of Mother Theresa,[4] it was revealed that for a time when she was called to establish the mission of the Sisters of Charity, she felt a very vibrant relationship with, and call from, God who empowered her to move ahead. But then God went silent with her, and for years she felt totally bereft of any comfort or sustenance from the presence of God at work in her life.

---

[3] I speak at greater length on the idea of call having to be validated by the community faith in a later section of this chapter, "The Authority of the Bible." We note that we cannot isolate our discernment from the test of that of the wider community.

[4] Mother Theresa, *Come Be My Light*, ed. Brian Kolodiejchuk, M.C. (New York: Image-Doubleday, 2007).

Sola Scriptura

In a lecture given in 1989, N.T. Wright said that the authority of Scripture begins with the authority of God.[5] Authority begins and ends with God, and we witness it in a series of deeds: God creates the heavens and the earth, Abraham is called, the Exodus unfolds, the Exile takes place, the Exiles return. In the New Testament God's authority is vested fully in Jesus Christ, then through the Holy Spirit to the apostles and then the Church. The Church then is "given authority to work within God's world as his accredited agent(s)."[6]

The actual Scripture itself is God-given. It originated with God and was given, God-breathed, through vessels chosen by God who filtered the revelation of God through history and literature, story and prophecy, and then given to the people of God. This Word, then under the same Holy Spirit, brought God's revelation together into a sacred whole so that the people of God could read, interpret, and understand it for their edification. It is by that same Holy Spirit that the Scripture is interpreted for our lives and for our churches.

The authority of Scripture comes out of its origination with God, and that it comes to us through a God-guided process. I would believe it to be, in its original form, inerrant, and sufficient for every need that we might have. Baptists believe that Scripture is the only authority from which we are to draw the truths for our lives. *Sola Scriptura,* Scripture alone says it all.

Problems with Scripture

Having an authority in the Bible, we must learn how to interpret it; this means that we develop a hermeneutic, or a style of reading the Bible and discovering the truths that shape our lives. It means that we have to face some difficult questions in interacting with the biblical content and text as we have it.

Certainly in our reading of the Bible we find that there are questions that come to all of our minds. Fred Craddock told the story of an early

---

[5] N.T. Wright, "How Can The Bible Be Authoritative?" The Laing Lecture 1989 and the Griffith Thomas Lecture 1989. Originally published in *Vox Evangelica 21* 1991, 7–32.

[6] Ibid., 7.

Sunday school lesson on the Christmas story when the teacher was talking about the poverty of the family of Jesus. She talked at length about how Mary and Joseph had to sleep in the stable and put Jesus into a manger, and then when they brought him to Jerusalem to be dedicated, they gave the poorest of the poor offerings, two doves. Craddock said he asked if they were so poor, what had happened to "all that gold, frankincense, and myrrh that the wise men brought?" He said the teacher looked at him and said, "We're not supposed to question the Bible." [7]

But we do. We question it dozens, if not hundreds of times when a dissonance or problem of a "feeling of something not right" jumps off the page at us.

Billy Graham tells the story of a time when he was attending Bible School in Florida and was struggling with the authenticity of the Bible. One day he was wrestling with the subject and made a simple declaration that he would never again question the Bible. He affirms that all of his life he has stayed true to that promise.[8]

I would give anything if I could be that way, but that is not my temperament. My mother would probably tell you that some of the first questions that came from my mouth were "Why?" and "How?" I wanted to know why there are two creation stories in Genesis instead of one. I wanted to know the value of the story where Lot fathered children with his own two daughters. I wanted to know how David could be such a complete scoundrel and yet still able to write the Psalms. Consequently, I struggle with two major problems with Scripture; the first is the text itself, and the second is what I call the Bible's lack of clarity.

Biblical Literalism

There are many who sincerely believe that the Bible should be interpreted literally, as it is. This is a very strong tenet of biblical fundamentalism, and is an extremely popular in most evangelical circles.

Literalists would reject any movement beyond a strict interpretation such as we find in more modern scholarship. This would articulate that

---

[7] Fred Brenning Craddock, *Reflections on My Call to Preach: Connecting the Dots*, (St Louis MO: Chalice Press, 2009) 77.

[8] This story is taken from my memory. I believe that originally it was found in *Just As I Am: The Autobiography of Billy Graham* (New York: HarperCollins, 1997).

the Bible was intended to be narrative, story, and metaphor—that it was never intended to be taken as straight history. Finding a similar story of the flood in the more ancient Babylonian Gilgamesh epic, which is clearly mythic, they would say is an example of this fact. One of the more popular advocates of a non-literalist approach would be the writing of Marcus Borg. He writes that the creation stories found in Genesis 1 and 2 are incompatible with each other and, therefore, cannot be history. He would question the historical accuracy of the first eleven chapters of Genesis. He questions the resurrection narrative of Jesus and claims that it was never expected to be taken as actual fact; in actuality it is a metaphor like many religious stories of its time pointing to a far deeper meaning. He would argue that it doesn't have to be factual to be true or meaningful.[9]

On the other hand, "Biblical literalists believe that, unless a passage is clearly intended as allegory, poetry, or some other genre, the Bible should be interpreted as literal statements by the author."[10] They would accept as factual the creation story, the flood, the long lives of the patriarchs, the history of Israel as recorded, the New Testament miracles of Jesus, the death and resurrection of Jesus, and the ascension of Jesus into heaven.

Literalism does not necessarily mean uniformity in Biblical understanding, and there are several different manifestations of literalism itself. It would be safe to say that the extremes of biblical literalism and biblical modern scholarship as suggested by Borg can be a sore test to Soul Freedom and an understanding of Biblical Authority.

The Text Itself

I said above that I have two major problems with the Scripture, the first problem being with the Biblical text itself. When I am teaching my course on Baptist Polity and we are speaking about the authority of Scripture, I ask my students to turn to the Gospel of John, chapter eight.

---

[9] Two of his books are: Marcus J. Borg, *Meeting Jesus Again for the First Time* (San Francisco: HarperSanFrancisco, 1994), and Marcus J. Borg, *Jesus: Uncovering the Life, Teachings, and Relevance of a Religious Revolutionary,* (San Francisco: HarperSanFrancisco, 1989).

[10] Wikipedia, "Biblical Literalism." http://en.wikipedia.org/wiki/Biblical_literalism

We make note of the fact that, in many modern editions of the Bible, the story of the woman caught in adultery has been inserted as a footnote instead as part of the text, with the explanation that the earliest original biblical manuscripts do not contain this story.

Then I turn to my Nestle Greek New Testament[11] and show them the footnotes on every single page with all of the variant readings found in different textual documents. The "best" reading according to Nestle is always found in the text, but the variants are real and must be considered. We talk about the ancient scribal way of copying the Scriptures, and how easy it was to lose lines, change letters, add explanatory notes to help the reader, or change something that an unsophisticated reader might misinterpret and be led into a view inconsistent with Church teaching.

Here we also speak of the fact that we have no original biblical manuscripts, so that the hundreds of translations are copies of copies. We illustrate the difficulties with the Isaiah 7:14 passage, where the King James Version announces, based on the translation of the Greek text, that "a virgin shall conceive," whereas the Revised Standard Version, based on the Hebrew, announces that "the young woman is with child."[12]

In 1892, Agnes Smith Lewis and Margaret Smith Gibson, twin sisters, discovered one of the oldest copies of the four gospels, written in Syriac, in a dark closet hidden in the Saint Catherine Monastery at the base of Mount Sinai.[13] It was one of the most stunning achievements in the history of biblical manuscripts. Agnes Smith Lewis had learned the Syriac language early on, and her sister later joined her in proficiency. [14]

---

[11] Eberhard Nestle, *Novum Testamentum Graece*, Massachusetts Bible Society, Boston.

[12] Isaiah 7:14, NRSV.

[13] This story is told in Janet Soskice's *The Sisters of Sinai: How Two Lady Adventurers Discovered the Hidden Gospels* (New York: Alfred A. Knopf, 2009).

[14] In the years following the discovery, male scholars had great difficulty in believing that Agnes Smith Lewis understood the difficult biblical language of Syriac, and that she would have recognized what she had in her hand for what it really was. Others who later told stories around the discovery made themselves more important and turned Lewis into a bystander. But the facts are inconvertible: she had been tipped off by a friend. She and her sister made the lengthy trip to Sinai—at that time ten days on a camel across the desert. She knew that she

Commenting on the texts, Agnes spoke against the dictation view of Scripture held by the many in the European Church at this time, that God dictated word for word the text of the King James Bible. Of this she said: "No one who has ever read two out of the 3829 MSS (of the New Testament) and has observed the many slight variations in the order of their words...can continue to hold this theory for a single moment. She then went on to describe one passage, with thirteen variations on the phrase "Jesus answered and said unto him":

Jesus answered, and said unto him,
Jesus answering, said unto him,
Jesus answered him, saying,
Jesus said unto him,
Jesus answered, saying,
Jesus, answering, said,
And Jesus said unto him,
And Jesus said,
Jesus said,
Jesus answered, and said,
And Jesus answering, said unto him,
And Jesus answered him, saying,
And Jesus answered, saying,[15]

Finally I ask my class to turn to the Gospel of Mark and look at what are known as the different endings of Mark.[16] There are nine of them with all of the variations, but the most significant differences are demonstrated

---

should look in a closet, and there she found a book that time had glued together. The sisters steamed the pages apart, and found it to be an ancient document that had been written over with lives of female martyrs. Agnes Smith Lewis could see enough of the underlying writing and understand it to be an early copy of the four gospels. The sisters then went ahead and took more than a thousand photographic images of the text, along with a number of other Syriac texts they found. It was an unprecedented achievement.

[15] Soskice, *The Sisters of Sinai*, 198–99. We note that none of the variations in this instance affected the substance of the text.

[16] See, for example Michael W. Holmes, "The Endings of the Gospel of Mark," in *Bible Review* (August 2001).

by the text, which ends with verse eight, and the other text that has the longer ending, going to verse twenty. The second ending is the ending that includes these admonitions: "And these signs will accompany those who believe: by using my name they will cast out demons: they will speak in new tongues: they will pick up snakes in their hands, and if they drink any deadly thing, it will not hurt them; they will lay their hands on the sick, and they will recover" (Mk 16:17–18). What we do, how we live our life of faith, is determined in some part by which of these texts we choose as Scripture. Obviously the second and longer text leads some into activity, some of which is not found elsewhere in Scripture.[17]

As we consider these variant texts we can learn a lot from the conclusions drawn by Agnes Smith Lewis in her book *Light on the Four Gospels*. The Smith sisters had grown up in the very stern Scottish Presbyterian Church, and they were Calvinistic to their core. They did not doubt at all the authority of Scripture or its ability to speak God's truth; but they were intrigued with the variant readings and asked "the question of why God should allow variants and scribal errors to creep into biblical manuscripts."[18] Recognizing that "we are not flawless automatons, and generations of scribes were bound to make mistakes,"[19] Agnes Smith Lewis concluded that "the very variants which frighten the weak-minded amongst us act as a stimulant to others, inciting them to search the Scriptures more diligently..."[20] We affirm this to be a hopeful truth.

Now, let me provoke you a little bit again with a contrarian view from Bart Ehrman's book *Misquoting Jesus*:

---

[17] We note that the ancient manuscript found by Agnes Smith Lewis and Margaret Smith Gibson at Saint Catherine's Monastery has the short ending, ending at verse eight, and there is no evidence of a missing page, for after a line the manuscript immediately starts the Gospel of Luke.

[18] Janet Soskice, *The Sisters of Sinai: How Two Lady Adventurers Discovered the Hidden Gospels* (New York: Alfred A. Knopf, 2009) 276.

[19] Ibid.

[20] This quote was originally from Agnes Smith Lewis's book *Light On the Four Gospels*; I have quoted it from the book by Janet Soskice, *The Sisters of Sinai: How Two Lady Adventurers Discovered the Hidden Gospels*, 276.

> The Bible began to appear to me as a very human book. Just as human scribes had copied, and changed, the texts of scripture, so too had human authors originally *written* the texts of scripture. This was a human book from beginning to end. It was written by different human authors at different times and in different places to address different needs. Many of these authors no doubt felt they were inspired by God to say what they did, but they had their own perspectives, their own beliefs, their own views, their own needs, their own desires, their own understandings, their own theologies; and these perspectives, beliefs, views, needs, desires, understandings, and theologies informed everything they said.[21]

My purpose in all of this is, simply, to get my students, and now us, to think about what these variant readings might mean to us. How do we find an authoritative text? What is the danger of establishing polity and authority on a variant text that might not be original? Is it possible for the Bible to become an idol to us? How do we probe beneath the surface? Which variant do we consider to be God's Word for us?

The Lack of Clarity

Then the second problem with the Scripture is what I call a lack of clarity with some of what we find in the Bible. We could also call this "proof-texting" or "picking and choosing."

Many years ago I was working with a pastoral intern who was attending Gordon-Conwell Theological Seminary. He was looking at ordination and was trying to decide if he would go with the Baptists or with the Presbyterians. As we talked about it we agreed that a good process would be for him to look seriously at the Scripture and see what the Bible had to say about baptism and let that be the guide for his career path in ordained ministry.

I, of course, knew that it was a slam-dunk, for I knew what the Bible said about baptism, for I had made my own study and concluded that baptism by immersion was the biblical model. I was therefore stunned—absolutely and completely stunned—when a month later the intern

[21] Bart D. Ehrman, *Misquoting Jesus* (San Francisco: HarperSanFrancisco, 2005) 11–12.

announced that he would become a Presbyterian, because that is where the Bible led him on the issue.

I have thought about that over the years, and I have come to realize that the Bible leads us to different conclusions on a number of matters. To put it another way, two people reading the Bible, and here I mean seriously and deliberately, prayerfully and thoughtfully, can come to completely different conclusions on a number of different matters. This is our experience; we know it to be a common event. Baptism is one of those subjects. Divorce is another. The role of women in ministry is yet another. Others include: homosexuality, abortion, the institution of slavery, and how we view eschatology.

The Authority of the Bible

You might remember that I said at the end of the section on *Sola Scriptura*: "We would believe (the Bible) to be, in its autograph, its original form, inerrant, and sufficient for every need which we might have."

I believe that the Bible in its original form was God's Word to us, that it was inspired writing, God-breathed in fact, to those who wrote it and who pulled it together into a textual whole. To suggest that the Bible we have today is equal to the original is to make it into an idol. Our task is to find out what God has in it to say to us and to the Church, and I believe that there is a process for that discernment. Of this Walter Brueggemann said: My discoveries of the Bible "come through the writing and witness of people who are empowered by the text to live lives of courage, suffering and sacrifice, people who have found this book a source and energy for the fullness of true life lived unafraid."[22]

This then is the process of study and interpretation.

The first step is study of the text, and by study I mean serious study, with the Greek and the Hebrew (if possible), and with commentaries from across the ages on the text and its meaning. This is the work of the pastor and preacher in their daily devotional practice, and certainly in the diligent preparation for preaching. It is this result, out of that deep,

[22] Walter Brueggemann, "Biblical Authority," in *The Christian Century* (3–10 January 2001): 13–20.

thoughtful, and prayerful study that should be delivered and interpreted on Sunday morning. The people of God deserve nothing less.

The second step is prayer, constant prayer if you will, as the text and the commentaries are open before us. We are asking the Holy Spirit to guide our thoughts, our research, our insights, our declarations, and our conclusions. One of the most powerful resources I have found for this is the process of *Lectio Divina*, or "praying the Scriptures." I have found that it helps me focus; more importantly it gives me some breathing room. We can get so intense sometimes that we lose sight of the whole as we try to concentrate on the parts. When I stop and wait upon God, when I take a text and ask God to reveal its meaning to me, when I sit in the silence and wait for God to speak, more often than not I am astounded at what bubbles up from the depths of my being. Absent the Holy Spirit, our study is no more than bubbling ideas; with the Holy Spirit it becomes revelation, God's Word for us today in time and place. A significant discovery for me was that the same passage or passages would sometimes have different meanings to me at different times; more than once I found that God had a special Word for me that was very applicable to something with which I was dealing at the time, but another day God might give me another Word out of it to match the particular needs of that day and its circumstances.[23]

The third factor of study is the group process of the Church. Let me give an example: There came a time in my life when I believed that I had a call to Christian ministry. I remember how affirming my mother was with that decision and how she said that she certainly was not surprised. My father never said much, but I learned later that he regularly kept those with whom he worked at the Boston Edison Company apprised of my progress. "I went through college and seminary with you," said one of his co-workers. I remember my grandmother, Jessie Doughty, giving thanks to God for my decision. I remember that my friends were not at all surprised, or if they were they kindly did not let on to me that they were. It was more "we could see it coming," (though there were a few, I confess, who were completely stunned—obviously they did not know me

---

[23] A resource that was of extreme importance to me in learning this discipline was: M. Basil Pennington, *Lectio Divina: Renewing the Ancient Practice of Praying the Scriptures* (New York: The Crossroad Publishing Company, 1998).

as well). I remember talking to my pastor, Fred Knox, who affirmed my gifts, and the next thing I knew I was scheduled to preach at the morning worship service and the church was voting to give me a License to Preach the Gospel. Especially moving was a comment by Mrs. Larsen. She had known me all of my life, and had watched me grow up in that church. As she was going out of church one morning she took my hand and she said with a twinkle in her eye and with heartfelt expression: "I'm not surprised." That's all we need, isn't it!

What might I have done if any one of them had said to me, "We don't see it. We don't see you having those gifts." It surely would have sent me back to the drawing board to reconsider the evidence and my feelings.

This process has a wider institutional bearing. During the seventies I chaired what then was called the Ministerial Preparation Committee for the American Baptist Churches of Massachusetts. All candidates for ordination had to appear before my committee, and I can remember how painful it was when we had to say to a candidate, "We do not see evidence of your sense of call, at least at this time." It was a heavy responsibility, and yet a necessary filter if the ordination was to be recognized beyond the local church. But such a process is the means of discernment.

What I am saying is that, although I came to a conclusion about God's call in my life, that call was affirmed and reaffirmed by those in the church who had lived with me and known me most of my life. It was then affirmed by the wider church—by the local association, the state judicatory, and the national denomination. It is that kind of confirmation and affirmation that tells us that the intention is real, that the call does not come in a vacuum, but it comes in real life and time and in the midst of real people. The church confirmation is the validation.

Looking back, that is a rather long analogy, but my point is that my absolute conviction that the study of Scripture works exactly that same way. We study with the commentaries, we invite the Holy Spirit into our process, and then we bring what we believe to be our God-inspired thoughts, ideas, and conclusions to the church. This could be an interpretation of a passage; it could mean a mandate for the individual or the church; it could be about a life call, or a call for a particular ministry, or for a mission; it could involve goals and mission for the church. "Such attentiveness may lead us to recognize that the story of someone else's nurture in the faith could be a transformative gift that allows us to read the text in a new way.'[24]

As I, or as we, bring what I have studied and gathered and concluded to this body of believers, I bring it with the preconception that all of them, these people who are walking the journey with me, have been involved in the same kind of process. Out of it they share their thoughts and conclusions, and where they are similar we rejoice and where they are different we talk and we pray again and we go back to the text and out of all of this I believe that we discern the will of God and the truth of Scripture in that very real time and place for very real purposes.

"Decisions about biblical meanings are not made on the spot, but result from the growth of habits and convictions. And if that is so, then the disputes over meaning require not frontal arguments but long-term pastoral attentiveness to one another in good faith."[25]

The Authority of Scripture and Soul Freedom

If you are saying to yourself: "Aha! He's gotten off the Authority of Scripture and moved on to Soul Freedom" you are perceptive and exactly right.

To me, Soul Freedom and the Authority of Scripture are in lockstep with each other.[26]

Go back to the process. Study, then open yourself to the Holy Spirit, then share your conclusions with the church, and then go back again and again, recreating that circle.

Once, I was in a discussion with an individual on the issue of homosexuality and the Bible. We had come to different conclusions, and I

---

[24] Ibid., 3.

[25] Ibid.

[26] The genesis of this concept of Soul Freedom and the Authority of Scripture in lockstep was given to me originally by James M. Dunn. For many years James was the director of the Baptist Joint Committee on Public Affairs in Washington, D.C. and he has been over the decades a noted advocate, in all Baptist circles and before seats of government, of Soul Freedom and Separation of Church and State Issues. Some of his thought is articulated in a recent biography: Aaron Douglas Weaver, *James M. Dunn and Soul Freedom* (Macon: Smyth and Helwys Publishing, Inc., 2011).

said that the only way through this would be a belief in Soul Freedom, our ability to come to independent decisions on what the Bible teaches. He looked at me and said, "Soul Freedom must bow to Biblical Authority!" "Mine or yours?" I asked. He wanted to make Biblical Authority (or his view of it) normative—which was unacceptable to me—and he wasn't about to accept the fact that my conclusion might be normative.

In recent years my American Baptist denomination has been split over the homosexuality issue; through it all I have found that there is no working through the issue with those taking a strong, if not dogmatic, Biblical Authority stance, as they will not accept the Soul Freedom argument as equal to Biblical Authority. To them, Soul Freedom must be subservient. For those who believe in Soul Freedom, however, the difference of opinion is more grist for the mill, but it is understood that the process must be kept open and be continuous. In the end we have to agree to disagree; the only other option is schism.

We do believe that the kingdom of God is large enough for those who look differently at Biblical Authority. The problem, again, is when those arguing the preeminence of Biblical Authority do not accept a Soul Freedom interpretation difference as acceptable, they are not open to diversity of interpretation in many texts.

In the midst of my denomination's struggle with the homosexuality issue, I happened to have a meeting with a long time friend, Kent Millard. Kent was the senior minister of St Luke's United Methodist Church in Indianapolis, which I believe is the largest Methodist Church north of the Mason-Dixon Line. Kent gave me an analogy that has stuck with me. He said to picture a large diamond in the middle of a room, with a light shining directly over it. A circle of people surrounds the diamond, and they see the light through one of the facets that face them. He noted that a diamond has many facets, yet it is a single piece of crystal. He encouraged me to see the Bible as that diamond, a single unit with many facets that are lit by God. The Bible is seen through those different facets by individuals, each of who might come to a different conclusion about the same book because they are focusing through their individual window of perception—yet all are looking at the same Bible.[27]

The Authority of Scripture is real; it guides our lives as we seek God's revelation for us in it. It is sufficient for doctrine and salvation. And it is my truth—your truth—and together, our truth.[28]

Biblical Authority and the Pulpit

I believe that good Biblical scholarship and preaching is central to life within a local Baptist church. In my thinking, a strong church will have a variety of viewpoints on biblical matters sitting in the congregation. In my opinion, diversity is central to who we are—the truest playing out of Soul Freedom. Preaching from the pulpit should be strong enough to challenge the thinking of the congregation, and consistent enough to bring continuity to the process of interpretation. The preacher who enters the pulpit absent time and scholarship in the study does a disservice to himself or herself, and even more so to the members of the congregation. Biblical scholarship should be a commandment for ordination and a life in ministry.

Architecturally, Baptist churches have traditionally been structured to emphasize the preaching of the Word. The pulpit, in most cases, is central to the platform, a statement to the fact that proclamation or teaching is of utmost importance. It is set up much like a classroom with students or congregation seated in rows before the person speaking to them. A split chancel with a lectern and a pulpit is equally affirmative, with the Word of God read from the lectern and the proclamation and interpretation of the Word of God from the pulpit. There is some

---

[27] "Soul Freedom is obviously involved in these differences of interpretations, but so is hermeneutics. Both sides are committed to Biblical Authority but don't share the same hermeneutic." This comment was made by Dennis Johnson, senior minister of Baptist Temple in Charleston, West Virginia. Johnson observed this while editing this manuscript. Biblical hermeneutics is the "science and methodology" of interpreting Biblical text (American Heritage Dictionary).

[28] Resources for this chapter include: Jon H. Armstrong, "The Authority of Scripture," *Sola Scriptura! The Protestant Position on the Bible*, ed. Don Kistler (Orlando FL: Soli Deo Gloria Publishers, 1997). "Baptist Beliefs," Wikipedia. http://en.wikipedia.org/wiki/Baptist_beliefs

suggestion that the split chancel originated in the idea that the reading of the Word and the preaching of the Word should be separated to clarify the difference between them, one authentic, the other interpretative.

Topics for Discussion

Biblical Authority Scenario 1

You are in dialogue with another Baptist, one who is known to have more conservative views than you do. You are discussing one of the more significant social issues of the day—perhaps slavery, divorce, women in ministry, or homosexuality—and he keeps saying to you "But the Bible says...," or "Leviticus tells us...," or "the Apostle Paul said when he wrote to the Corinthians...." You allow that you interpret the Scripture a bit differently than he does, and you speak to him about Soul Freedom—that is the right and privilege of the believer to go to the Scripture and, with their conscience and the power of the Holy Spirit, come to a conclusion as to what it means to them and to their lives. When you finish this statement he says sternly, "Biblical Authority must trump Soul Freedom." Hearing that, you finally say to him, "But consider the endings to the Gospel of Mark."

Discussion Questions for Scenario 1

1. Could you be another Billy Graham and state that never again will you ask questions about the Bible?
2. What do the nine endings to the Gospel of Mark say to you about the authority of the Bible?
3. How do you personally resolve questions about the biblical text and Biblical Authority?
4. In your most honest moments, how do you resolve the fact that very serious students of the Bible come to very different conclusions about what the Bible says on a variety of different topics?
5. Do you believe that Biblical Authority and Soul Freedom are in lockstep with each other, to be given equal value in our interpretations? Or do you believe that Soul Freedom should bow to Biblical Authority? Or do you believe that Biblical Authority should bow to Soul Freedom?

6. Some would say that while there are many variants in the Scriptural text, none are sufficiently "different" so as to affect doctrine and / or belief. Do you agree with that?
7. How do you find absolute truth in Scripture, truth that will satisfy your own life needs?
8. What would you say to an individual who says that the variants in the Biblical text are enough to keep them from seeing it as truth, and thus from becoming a Christian?
9. What do you mean by inerrancy?

Biblical Authority Scenario 2

A member of your board of deacons, known to be in a troubled marriage, went on a church-sponsored trip to Israel. You notice him becoming increasingly friendly with a divorced woman in the group—interestingly a deaconess—and when they return home you begin to notice that they are often seen together around the church. Next you hear that he has announced that he is divorcing his wife so that he can marry his new friend.

Discussion Questions for Scenario 2

1. Do you say, "Congratulations—I know you have found happiness with each other"?
2. Do you say, "I think we may have a problem here"?
3. How does this relate to what the apostle had to say about the qualifications to be a deacon in 1 Timothy 3?
4. Should a divorced woman be a deaconess? Should a divorced person hold any office in the church?
5. This seems to be a strange intersection between Soul Freedom and Biblical Authority. Do you agree? Does one or the other take precedence? If so, then which one? If they are equal, do we, or does the church, have the right to question a decision that came out of their Soul Freedom to interpret the Scripture and be in relationship with each other?
6. What kind of implications does this relationship have within the life of the church? The church would be extremely judgmental? The church would be tolerant? The church would ignore the whole situation as in "live and let live"?

7. What kind of implications does this have for their status as a deacon and deaconess?
8. Should either of them be asked to resign their position? The deacon? The deaconess? Both?
9. What kind of action, if any, should the church take on their membership?
10. Should they be allowed to stay in the life of the church or is this a matter for church discipline?
11. Should the church have policies in place here on certain behaviors? If so, what should those behaviors be? With each behavior, what should the policy be?
12. Would the policies reflect a view in a hierarchy of sin? Or is all sin equal as in "sin is sin"?
13. Are there circumstances that would allow the church to treat each case individually, with consideration for extenuating conditions?

Commentary on Scenario 2

For another look at the issue of leadership and divorce within the Church, and from a different perspective, see Biblical Authority Scenario 4.

Biblical Authority Scenario 3

You observe that the chair of your church's Worship Committee has invited a lesbian couple and their children to be the family chosen to light the Advent candle for the fourth Sunday of Advent.

Discussion Questions for Scenario 3

1. What are your initial thoughts as you read this?
2. Do you say: "Well, this should be interesting." Or do you say, "Lord, deliver me!" or perhaps, "This is absolutely outrageous," or even, "Heads will roll!"?
3. Do you pat the worship leader on the back and thank them for being creative and inclusive?
4. Do you utter a mild cuss word (to yourself only of course)!
5. Do you call for the worship leader to resign?

6. Do you tell the worship leader they must undo the invitation immediately, no questions asked?
7. If the worship leader asks "Why?" (possibly questioning your authority or your judgment or both), how would you explain the decision to remove them to the lesbian couple?
8. Should the lesbian couple be excluded because they are in a relationship that you believe to be sinful according to your interpretation of the Scripture?
9. If you said yes to the above question, are there other "sins" which would also bring exclusion from participation? For example, divorce or being a member of a Masonic (secret) Order? How about those who are very overweight and guilty of gluttony? Known to be unforgiving in their personal relationships? Known to be very judgmental of others?
10. If you said yes to the view of Scriptural Authority saying that a lesbian relationship is sinful, is this a matter that should prevent them from staying involved in the life of the church?
11. Does your church have a policy on homosexuality and gay and lesbian people participating in the life of your church? If it doesn't, should it? What should it be?
12. What are the implications here for the life of your church?
13. Is it hypocritical to select one area of "sin" for exclusion and not others?
14. How do you feel personally about this? Are your feelings at variance with your church? Or are your feelings in accord with your church? If they are at variance, how does each side deal with divergent opinion (assuming it has been expressed)?
15. What do you think you personally would do? Why?
16. Do you think there would be repercussions? If so, what would they be?

Biblical Authority Scenario 4

A small, somewhat rural church was governed by a group of seven members of the church, with a couple of them re-elected every year. Because of the nature of the community there was not a lot of turnover, but eventually someone would move away or decide not to stand for re-election, and a vacant position would need to be filled. In the course of time, a vacancy did occur, and an individual in good standing within the congregation was nominated for the position. In the course of the discussion it was noted that the individual nominated had been divorced, and that church practice did not allow a divorced individual to serve as a leader. With that, someone called attention to the fact that there already was someone on the board who was divorced, so precedent had been set. However, it was pointed out that the divorced person on the board had been divorced "before he got saved" and the candidate had been divorced "after he had got saved," and it was felt that there was a substantial difference between the two.

Discussion Questions for Scenario 4

1. What is your initial reaction as you read this?
2. What is the Biblical Authority principle that applies to this situation?
3. How does your church feel about divorce?
4. Does your church allow divorced individuals to be church members?
5. Are there other practices that would exclude people from membership?
6. Are there other practices that would exclude people from leadership?
7. Would you remind those in opposition of the words of Jesus on judgment, "Let those who are without sin cast the first stone"?
8. If your church allows divorced members, do they allow divorced members in leadership?
9. What do you feel about the distinction between "before" and "after" salvation, as suggested in the above illustration? Do you find any Biblical Authority for such a view? What do you think the church's reasoning might be?
10. Would you recommend to a person ready to make a profession of faith that they do anything they want beforehand because God will wipe the slate clean (i.e. "Sin greatly that grace may abound!")?
11. ?
12. Is there a difference in God's world of forgiving sins differently before or after we claim faith? In other words, if a non-Christian

asks forgiveness, does God treat that request differently than God would treat a request from a Christian?

Biblical Authority Scenario 5

A young couple attending your church has a baby, and it is a time of great excitement for them and for their extended families. When you visit with them at the hospital, they raise the possibility of having the "baby dedicated." They ask you how soon that service should be held and when it would be possible to schedule it. You explain to them that it is really a service of parental dedication, in which the parents make a pledge to raise the child in "the nurture and admonition of the Lord." You explain further that as a part of the service you will bless them and the baby, and that the congregation will pledge their commitment to help you bear the broad responsibility of raising the child to adulthood and a time of personal Christian commitment.

Discussion Questions for Scenario 5

1. Do you think that a dedication service is an attempt to give Baptists a ceremony akin to infant baptism?
2. Why isn't the "Service of Parental Dedication" an ordinance like baptism and the Lord's Supper?
3. What is the Biblical background of such a service of dedication and blessing?
4. What kind of requirements do you have as a pastor for officiating at such a service? Do you believe that there should be restrictions? If so, what should they be?
5. What kind of requirements does the church itself have?
6. What would happen if your requirements to lead a service were different from the requirements established by the church?
7. Does anything change if the baby is not born naturally to these parents but was brought into their family through adoption?
8. Does anything change if only one of the parents is active in the life of the church?
9. Does anything change if neither of the parents is active in the life of the church?
10. Does anything change if neither of the parents is active in the life of the church, but one or both sets of grandparents are active?

11. Does anything change if the parents are a lesbian couple, one of who conceived the child through artificial insemination?
12. Does anything change if the couple is homosexual, with one of them having contributed sperm for artificial insemination?

Biblical Authority Scenario 6

You are at a time in your life when you are looking for a pastoral position in a church. You are open to move anywhere in the country, and you duly state this on your denominational personnel form. Your area minister tells you about a new program of "face-to-face" meetings set up by several regions at once in order to get churches and search committees together. This seems like a wonderful way to explore a number of open options, to meet with various churches, and to get to know regional and denominational staff. You attend, and the meetings seem to go well, and there is what you would call a "special magic" with one of the churches; you liked them very much and they seemed very responsive to you. It does not seem to stretch the truth when you tell your family upon returning home that you sense God opening a door for you. Later that week you receive a call from the executive minister of that region. They tell you that the church has been in contact with them and that indeed, they would like to begin further conversations. Then you are told that before the region can affirm your candidacy, they require that you sign a theological statement that states that you agree with their biblical interpretation that homosexuality is a sin, that homosexuals should not be active in leadership within a church, and that homosexuals should not be ordained or given opportunities for ministry.

Discussion Questions for Scenario 6

1. What are your initial thoughts as you read this? You are glad that someone is finally taking a stand? You are appalled at the terrible breech of the Soul Freedom principle? You feel that they have greatly overreached the Biblical Authority principle?
2. Is this the time to have a discussion with the regional minister about the practical applications of the Authority of Scripture?
3. Should you point out to them that there are differing views on the Bible and homosexuality?

4. Would you ask if this was the policy of the region, is it also the policy of the church that is interested in you?
5. Is it possible to go to the church and bypass the regional minister? If so, is that good politics, or polity, or practice?
6. How would you personally respond to this?
7. Would you sign the statement without believing it just to forward your name, thinking that it is neither a serious issue nor a "big deal"?
8. What are the issues for which it is worth drawing a line in the sand, where crossing that line would be too great an insult for your personal integrity:
9. Does this interfere with your concept of Soul Freedom? If so, how do you go about articulating that?
10. What does this requirement tell you about the openness of the region and the churches' ministry to all individuals? Is that conclusion problematic to you?
11. If one particular sin is restrictive to placement, are there others that should also be restrictive?
12. Is all sin the same, or is there a hierarchy of sins where some are more heinous than others?

Biblical Authority Scenario 7

You are at a national meeting of the general board of the denomination, and you happen to end up in conversations over dinner with someone you have seen around, but with whom you have never spoken personally. One of the issues being discussed by the board is that of homosexuality, and he raises the issue. "Why are we talking about this?" he asks. "The Bible says it is a sin and that should be enough for us!"

You hesitate, wondering if you really want to go down this path, the gate to which he has opened. But you take a deep breath, and you say, "Which Bible—my Bible or your Bible?"

"The Bible is clear," he says, obviously missing the point you subtly had tried to raise, that of people interpreting the Bible in different ways.

You realize that you will have to be more direct. "I interpret the Bible a little differently than you do on this matter; I think that the Bible is more open on the subject than what you are allowing. You know that Jesus never addressed the issue; he spent his time talking about the use of money, about forgiveness, and about loving enemies and those who persecute you."

So it is that you go back and forth over the meal—point, counterpoint. Finally, as you finish dessert, he picks up his tray, smiles at you, and tells you that he has enjoyed the conversation, though he is surprised that any Christian could hold such views as those you had expressed. Then he says, "You are a really nice person. But (pause) you know (pause) with your view (pause) you are going to hell!" And with that he walks away.

Discussion Questions for Scenario 7

1. What is your initial reaction as you read this?
2. What are the Baptist Principle issues in this conversation? How does it reflect on Biblical Authority? How does it reflect on Soul Freedom? Which principle does each of those in the conversation hold pre-eminent?
3. What do you think?

—You were crazy to even be in this conversation?

—You want to tell him that you are glad God will judge you in the last day, instead of him.

—You decide to change the focus of the issue—you call him stupid and start yelling at him.

—You wonder if you might have misread the Scripture.

—You want to give him a lecture on the Baptist view of Soul Freedom and the Priesthood of the individual believer, not to mention the *real* nature of Biblical Authority.

—You are glad for his evangelical zeal.

—You want to go home, get down on your knees, and have a good cry.

4. As you sat there enjoying your coffee after he left, what would you be feeling?
5. Do you think that Jesus might have had a similar feeling, like what you are feeling, after one of his conversations with the Pharisees?

Biblical Authority Scenario 8

Searching for a new pastor for their church, the pastoral search committee was in a lively discussion around the qualifications of some individuals represented in the profiles they had received from the American Baptist Personnel Service. Raising some special heat was the fact that several of the profiles were those of women seeking pastoral positions. One of the more active, though traditional, members said that the Bible clearly states that there were prohibitions against a woman having authority over men, and that men should not be taught by women.

A more moderate member of the committee tried to give an alternative view. He mentioned Romans 16:7 where Paul sends greetings to "Andronicus and Junia," whom he calls "my relatives who were in prison with me; they are prominent among the apostles, and they were in Christ before I was" (Rom 16:7). Clearly "Junia is a woman," said the moderate member, "and was recognized by Paul as one of the apostles." He concluded by saying: "If the Bible is ambiguous as it sometimes is, if it is situational as it sometimes is, if it suggests one thing in one place and another in another place as it sometimes does, how then can we interpret it so authoritatively and so narrowly on such a topic as this?"

Discussion Questions for Scenario 8

1. What are your initial thoughts as you read this?
2. In the quote above regarding Junia, what do you think the moderate is trying to say? What do your ears hear as he speaks? What does your heart feel as he speaks? What does this illustration say to you about Biblical Authority? What does this illustration say to you about Soul Freedom?
3. What are some other areas of the Bible where different sides form regarding interpretation of particular texts? How do we get around or through these divergent, often radically so, interpretations?
4. What do you believe about the possibility of women in ministry? Why do you believe that?
5. What do you do with the arguments on the negative side of the issue? The Bible does say that women should not teach men. The Bible does say that women should not have authority over men. The Bible does say that women should keep silent within the church.

6. Speaking to the issue that there are still major Baptist denominations that still do not allow women in the pulpit: What do you say to them? Do you give them a "Praise the Lord! Hold firm!" Do you tell them that they need to go back to the commentaries? Do you need to bring them up on the latest Biblical Scholarship?
7. What would you say to the woman who sincerely feels that God has spoken to her with a call to ministry? Can such a call be authentic? Or is she delusional?
8. What does this say about the perils of biblical interpretation?
9. What is the process we take for interpreting the Bible collectively as a church? In this context how do we deal with differences? How can the two individuals on the search committee reconcile and more forward?
10. The corporate world speaks of career women hitting "glass ceilings." How would this apply here?

Commentary on Scenario 8

Many of the scenarios transcend several different Baptist Principles, and this reflects deeply on the fact that they are overlapping, as they relate to one another. The following illustration clearly shows that intertwining—it has elements of Biblical Authority, the Priesthood of the Individual Believer, and Soul Freedom.

When I reached seminary in the fall of 1962, I do not recall ever having done any serious thinking about the issue of women in ministry. Nor do I recall knowing any women ministers. At the time, Gordon Divinity School (now Gordon-Conwell Theological Seminary) was virtually all male. Any women involved were either on a Christian Education track, or were married to future ministers and/or missionaries, and wanted to pick up some courses to be better helpmates to their husbands. One of my strongest memories was the maleness of the singing in chapel; it was always robust, of course, as we loved to sing the great hymns of the Church. Any female voices were in the minority and easily overwhelmed by weight of numbers. We sadly did not think about it at the time, but retrospectively it was an interesting symbol of life at the seminary at that time.

In January of 1963, Nelson Elliott, who was Field Education Director, pulled me aside one day and spoke to me about a situation that had just come to his attention. First Baptist Church of Gardner, Massachusetts, was looking for a student intern; would I be interested? Then he hesitated before saying, "The church has a woman minister. Would that make a difference?"

Well, I didn't think it would. At least I did not think negatively enough to keep me from talking to the church and the pastor about the possibilities and the ministry being offered. Her name was the Reverend Ruth Elizabeth Thompson, and everyone called her either "Betty" or "Mrs. Thompson." After the meeting, Connie and I decided that we liked her, we liked the church, and we found that they liked us enough to offer us the position. I'm not sure I ever thought about any biblical prohibition; I saw the practical considerations: For a two-hour drive each way and a commitment for Saturday and Sunday every week, they were going to pay me thirty dollars—twenty-five for salary and five for gas money.

My classmates did make a statement, however. On Valentine's Day of 1963 I walked into the mailroom of Gordon Divinity School to be greeted by a most pungent odor. Imagine my surprise when I discovered that it emanated from my mailbox. There in the box was an envelope with a valentine in it that had been totally saturated in the cheapest perfume that the local drugstore had available. And, surrounded with hearts, it was signed "with love from your pastor." All of my friends, of course, loved the prank and thought the card was hilarious.

I discovered quickly that Betty Thompson was one of the most gifted preachers, one of the finest pastors I had ever had the privilege to meet. I learned an enormous amount about church and ministry from her. Because of her it never occurred to me that women would be denied a call to ministry, as I had met and worked with one who was more gifted and effective than many of the male pastors I was to meet in the years to come. She was head and shoulders above the rest.

One final observation of interest to me—for it relates to what was to be my future ministry—is that at the end of the day on Sunday, as Connie and I prepared for the drive back to our home in Manchester, Massachusetts, we would have a final cup of coffee and something to eat in the kitchen of the parsonage. Around that table Betty Thompson would tell us stories about people and relate incidents that had been part of her life experience growing up at First Baptist Church of Beverly, Massachusetts. It is one of God's great ironies that in the fall of 1964 I was called as the associate minister of the Beverly Church. I knew a good segment of the congregation by name from her stories, and I believe to this day that God had been preparing me.

As an aside, Betty's husband Tom worked for one of the major fund-raisers and spent weeks on the road conducting church capital fund campaigns. When he was home, I found it interesting to talk to him, and what I learned from Tom about fund-raising served me extremely well in the three churches I was to later serve.

Biblical Authority Scenario 9

The congregation is sitting comfortably in the pews on a Communion Sunday morning. The choir has been especially good singing the anthem, the prayers have seemed especially touching, and in a silent moment there is a rustle of anticipation as the pastor is about to rise and begin the sermon. Suddenly there is a commotion in the back, and all heads turn. The ushers are trying to restrain a man who is seeking to enter the sanctuary. It is obvious that he is very emotional and angry. He breaks loose and strides up the center aisle. You're not sure what he is saying, but you think you hear the words "You have turned my father's house into a den of thieves." When he reaches the front of the church he upends the communion table and the silver cup holders and bread trays go flying, landing with a clattering noise upon the hardwood floor. It may be your imagination but it seems like there is fire coming from his eyes. He pauses for a moment to look around; seizing the opportunity of respite, you jump from your seat and move forward to face him.

Discussion Questions for Scenario 9

1. Does it occur to you that this might be Jesus Christ?
2. Is it possible that you would think this person to be deranged?
3. What options run through your mind?
4. What might he say to your question "What are you doing?"
5. What might he say to your question "What or who gives you the right to this violence?"
6. Thinking this through, can you grasp how the Jewish leaders felt when Jesus claimed the authority to cleanse the temple?

6

The Lord's Supper

There are two ordinances within our Baptist church life; one is baptism, the other is the Lord's Supper. Baptists differentiate between sacraments and ordinances.

A sacrament is a ritual within the church that has a sacred aspect to it, for in it there is the imparting of God's grace. An ordinance is merely a remembrance or a memorial. Baptists believe the Lord's Supper to be "outward expression of faith" in "obedience to [Jesus] Christ."[1] There is no belief in the ordinance that the elements of communion themselves deliver a portion of God's grace.

The Lord's Supper comes out of the Passover meal observed by Jesus with his disciples on "the night when he was betrayed" (1 Cor 11:23), or the night before his death on the cross. During that shared meal, Jesus turned the bread and the cup into symbols of his body and blood. His words of institution can be found in Matthew 26:26–29, Mark 14:22–25, Luke 22:14–20, and Paul recaps it in 1 Corinthians 11:23–26.

Jesus told his disciples that in the future, at a time when he would no longer be with them, they would take the bread, break it, and eat it, they would take the cup and drink it, and that in doing this they would be remembering him. In the Corinthians passage, Paul quotes Jesus as stating that this act together was an act of declaration, a proclamation of his death, until such a time, in an eschatological statement, as he would return to them.

The act of bread and cup became a symbol of the presence of Jesus in our midst. Luke, in his gospel, follows the Easter story with an account of two disciples walking to Emmaus, and on this journey they fell into step with a stranger who seemed ignorant of the recent events surrounding the death of Jesus. They explained it all to him as they walked, and then when they reached their destination they invited him to stay with them. It was as they sat at the table and broke bread that they

---

[1] "Eucharist," Wikipedia. http://en.wikipedia.org/wiki/Eucharist

recognized the stranger to be Jesus; their eyes had been closed to that fact (Lk 24:31). I read this as a portrait of what is to come, for, historically, it has been in the act of breaking bread and drinking the cup that Jesus has been revealed to us in quiet but real ways.

After the death of Jesus, the early disciples would gather together in homes and share a meal remembering him. In that participation they felt very close to him, experiencing his nearness and presence with them. At first, when the church was small, it was a simple matter to get together. As the church became larger and more complex the meal took on new dimensions. We know from history that eventually the Church had to meet behind locked doors because of persecution;[2] we know that the Lord's Supper became somewhat institutionalized, for James spoke of honoring some people seated at the meal more than others, indicating that status was making some more equal than others (James 2:1–7). The Lord's Supper was becoming more than just a meal as it began to be joined with elements of worship and church.

Over the centuries, the Church developed the meal into the Mass and declared that through this act the bread and the wine, in some miraculous, mysterious way, became the body and blood of Jesus Christ. This transubstantiation could be accomplished only by a priest, and the meal could be celebrated only with a priest present and leading the worship.

The reformers rejected this belief in transubstantiation, of bread and wine becoming the real body and blood of Jesus. Martin Luther came part way, articulating what became known as consubstantiation; he said that while the elements did not actually become the real body and blood of Jesus, they contained the real presence of Jesus.

The reformers, in re-evaluating ancient and traditional practices, declared that the Agape Meal or Communion or Lord's Supper was a memorial to Jesus Christ. Those emerging as new leaders said that the bread and the cup were no more than that—bread and cup, but in the

---

[2] I would cite the story of Peter in Acts 12, who, when released from prison went immediately to the house of Mary, the mother of John Mark. Reaching the gate, he could not enter because it was locked, and the servant was so excited to see him she ran to tell the assembly without unlocking the gate.

symbol of what they represented they helped us to remember Jesus, to think upon his love and grace brought to us through the cross.

This became the Baptist viewpoint. The Lord's Supper is a memorial service that remembers Jesus and how he worked on our behalf. The Short Confession of 1610 stated that there are

> two sacraments[3] appointed by Christ, in his holy church, the administration whereof he hath assigned to the ministry of teaching, namely, the Holy Baptism and the Holy Supper. These are outward visible handlings and tokens, setting before our eyes, on God's side, the inward spiritual handling which God, through Christ, ... setteth forth.[4]

While the meaning and the intent of the Lord's Supper is fairly uniform amongst Baptist churches, there are numerous differences in style and practice which emerge out of theology, history, and culture.

Some churches practice the Lord's Supper as a closed communion; this means that only the baptized members of that particular church can participate, so as the communion hymn is sung all of the non-members are asked to quietly remove themselves from the sanctuary. Other churches will allow all Baptists to participate, but none from other non-Baptist church communions, and none who are not professing Christian believers. Many churches practice an open communion, in which they make it clear that the table is open to any and all who have made a profession of faith in Jesus Christ as their Lord and Savior. And there are some churches where it is open to any and all who want to participate.

Most use bread and grape juice; we are rooted in the temperance movements of several generations past. Very occasionally you will see a

---

[3] Baptists shy away from using the term "sacrament" to define Baptism and the Lord's Supper because "sacrament" implies to many the infusion of a magical power. We see experiencing the two more as an act of obedience to the commands of Jesus Christ. Norman Maring and Winthrop Hudson see some credibility in the use of "sacrament"; for a full discussion see Norman H. Maring and Winthrop S. Hudson, *A Baptist Manual of Polity and Practice*, rev. ed. (Valley Forge PA: Judson Press, 1991) 145–47.

[4] William L. Lumpkin, *Baptist Confessions of Faith* (Valley Forge PA: Judson Press, 1969) 119.

Baptist church that will use real wine. I know of youth meetings that have tried to contemporize the service by using more popular elements from the youth culture, for example Pepsi and pretzels, arguing that pretzels are bread indeed, and Pepsi can be served in a cup. To some, this practice is non-controversial; to others it is very controversial. The difficulty lies in the elements themselves. The cup, it is advocated, should be from the "fruit of the vine," which would mean either wine or grape juice. This most closely approximates what Jesus used in the upper room. The bread should ideally be unleavened bread as, again, that would most closely match that of the upper room, but leaven bread would fit somewhat in the category. I am not sure where other forms of breads such as bagels, doughnuts, or pastries would fit in; probably the non-traditionalists would be fine with such a choice, and the more traditional would see this as a step too far.

To my knowledge, most Baptist churches observe the ordinance of the Lord's Supper on the first Sunday of the month, though there are some who serve it quarterly, and some who serve it only on special occasions.

Generally it is an ordained minister who administers the Lord's Supper. "Baptists have usually insisted that an ordained person preside at the Communion service."[5] As I have researched this, it seems to be more functional than theological. Theologically, in fact, believing that we all are priests, there should be no exclusions. The greater issue is that the church must keep Communion from "being treated carelessly," that "due seriousness and reverence are shown toward the observance."[6] If someone other than an ordained minister is to lead the Communion it should be an individual vetted and chosen by the church itself who is "fitted in spirit, character, and ability to lead in this kind of service."[7]

I have served in churches where only males could serve the Lord's Supper. Part of this was in the history that only males could be deacons.[8]

---

[5] Maring and Hudson, *A Baptist Manual of Polity and Practice*, 169.

[6] Ibid.

[7] Ibid., 170.

[8] In an interesting twist, I remember hearing when I served the First Baptist Church of Malden, Massachusetts, that years previously, to be a deacon—in addition to being male—you also had to be a Mason, belonging to the local lodge. When I asked about it the logic was simple; the deacons at that time wore what

The male dominance has changed as the culture has changed. In all three of the churches in which I served, the deacons eventually became the diaconate, which combined what were the old deacons and deaconesses. Even within my own generation I can remember when the deaconesses could only prepare the Communion and clean up after it; they could not actually serve it.

I served as an associate minister from 1964 to 1977 at First Baptist Church of Beverly, Massachusetts. There the change to allowing women to participate in serving came about in an interesting way.

It started on a summer Sunday when the deacons (all male) could not muster four of their number to take the offering. One of the Deaconesses volunteered to assist, wondering if that would be all right. The answer seemed obvious; if they needed four to take the offering then they didn't seem to have much of a choice.

For summer services four deacons would come down the aisle, mount half a dozen steps to the platform, and stand in two columns to receive the offering plates. As Margaret Davey tells the story, "We walked down the aisle and we came up on to the platform George happened to be the only minister serving that Sunday; he looked at me with a raised eyebrow. I shrugged, he winked at me, and we went on took the offering." Once the barrier was broken it continued in following Sundays, and then there came the communion Sunday when there were insufficient deacons to serve, and it seemed most natural to include several members of the Deaconesses. Out of such innocent beginnings comes cataclysmic change![9]

The change has not always gone as easily. We know of instances where after long and passionate debate those serving the Lord's Supper continued to be entirely male. In other instances it has been cautiously and delicately changed, with good order, thoughtful theological discussion, and proper communication.

---

then were called morning coats—tuxedos with tails, and the only men in the church who would have such suits were the Masons who wore the morning suits to their Masonic meetings.

[9] Margaret Davey was the Deaconess member who took this forward step that Sunday. She told this story as a part of the 200th Anniversary Celebration of the First Baptist Church of Beverly.

When I came to First Baptist Church in Indianapolis in 1983, within a year we had, as a part of an overall restructuring, moved from two boards (deacon and deaconess) to a diaconate. When I retired in 2003, one of the stories told as they remembered my ministry was by Nell Duncan. Nell had grown up in a Southern Baptist church, and she could never remember seeing a woman serving the Communion. On a Sunday, sometime after the change in committee structure, when she was a full member of the diaconate, she was put into the rotation as a server. Nell said that some time had gone by because she personally found it difficult to make such a significant transition. But she was scheduled, and the Sunday arrived; as Nell tells this story one can tell that it is very emotional for her. It is at this point that her voice got very low and measured. She spoke of how apprehensive she was, and then in hushed tones, of what a holy moment that time became for her. It opened to her an entirely new way of thinking about herself as a Christian, and of the service that she could bring to her church.

In all of this I am trying to say that there is more in the celebration of the Lord's Supper than we think, and this is a part of the mystery inherent in it. I remember one awkward moment when the men and the women were serving the congregation and I closed my eyes in prayer. Some time later I heard several loud "Ahems," and as I opened my eyes the servers were standing there to hand back the trays to be placed on the table. I found out later that they had been standing there for a few minutes and I had not been aware of them. I also learned that they thought that I had fallen asleep and they didn't want to awaken me suddenly so as to alarm me, probably afraid of what I might have blurted out. In fact I had not fallen asleep; rather I was in the midst of one of those sacred moments that sometimes come upon us in worship, impervious to what was going on around me. I would suggest that we all need more such moments in church.

I use this to say that over the years Communion has become even more of a profound mystery to me. I don't understand it, but this I know: that it is a holy and precious time when in the quiet, prayer can become very important, and where in the prayer and reflection the presence of Jesus can be very real. I don't know why I am surprised, for Jesus did say that where two or three were gathered together he would be there in the midst, and this is a promise that I have found to be true.

Eating and Drinking Unworthily

In 1 Corinthians 11:27–28, the Apostle Paul gives an admonition: "Whoever, therefore, eats the bread or drinks the cup of the Lord in an unworthy manner will be answerable for the body and blood of the Lord. Examine yourselves, and only then eat of the bread and drink of the cup."

Many have accepted this literally and with fear and trepidation, not wanting to participate in the Lord's Supper, believing that only those who exist in a perfect state of righteousness are eligible. They put themselves through a rigorous self-examination each time with very intensive introspection that scrolls their slate of sin before heaven in hope that divine favor will erase it clean, allowing them to be worthy of participation.

Repentance and self-examination are very important to us all; it is a healthy spiritual practice to which we are called. At the same time, I have found that when I am the most unworthy, it is then that the Lord's Supper has meant the most to me. "Just as I am, without one plea, but that thy blood was shed for me, and that thou bidst me come to thee, O Lamb of God, I come, I come."[10]

A commentator suggests that being worthy and introspection are not what these verses from 1 Corinthians are about. Richard B. Hays suggests that the reference refers to verse 18 and that "to eat the meal unworthily means to eat it in a way that provokes divisions, with contemptuous disregard for the needs of others in the community." He goes on to say, "Paul's call to self-scrutiny must therefore be understood not as an invitation for the Corinthians to probe the inner recesses of their consciences but as a straightforward call to consider how their actions at the supper are affecting brothers and sisters in the church, the body of Christ."[11]

---

[10] The first stanza of Charlotte Elliott's famous hymn, "Just As I Am."

[11] Richard Hays, *Interpretation: A Bible commentary for Teaching and Preaching: First Corinthians* (Louisville KY: John Knox Press, 1997) 200.

Topics for Discussion

Lord's Supper Scenario 1

I am retired now. I am a participant in Communion, not a server. I am writing these words on a Sunday afternoon that also happens to be the first Sunday of the month. My mind goes back to this morning, to that experience of sitting in the pew preparing for the Lord's Supper. As he said the words of institution, the pastor looked around the congregation and stated clearly, "We practice an open table to which all are welcome, no matter your church background." My mind goes back further to other experiences, where the pastor would announce a hymn before the Lord's Supper so that those who were not active members in the life of that particular church could be excused, for the Lord's Supper was to be given solely to the faithful stewards of membership within the life of that individual body.

Discussion Questions for Scenario 1

1. What are the requirements for participating in the Lord's Table? For your church? For you as a pastor? For your denomination?
2. Is there a requirement for membership in the church?
3. Is there a requirement for baptism by immersion?
4. If a person is not a member of the church, should they have professed Jesus Christ as their Savior and Lord in order to receive the Lord's Supper?
5. Is the table open to an unbeliever as well? If not, how do you enforce the restriction?
6. What does the Scripture mean when it warns us not to unworthily participate in the table?
7. Does one have to prepare for participation in the Lord's Supper? If so, what might that require?
8. Jesus once said that if you are approaching the altar and bear something in your heart against someone else, you should leave your gift and go out, find the other individual, reconcile, and only then return to offer your gift (Mt 5:24). How would you relate the above passage to participation in the Lord's Supper?
9. Is there a requirement that the elements be bread and wine? Or that it be unleavened bread and wine? Or that it be grape juice

instead of wine? Would Pepsi-Cola and doughnuts be appropriate? What if the doughnuts had sprinkles on them?

10. What do you tell the mother who tells you that her six-year-old twins want to take the bread and cup as it passes by them, but that she has not allowed them to do that even though they persist and keep asking "why not?" What is your answer?

Lord's Supper Scenario 2

When introducing the Lord's Supper this morning, one thing that the pastor said was that by approaching the table, we are involved in a mystery. For some reason, that statement was an "Aha" moment for me—a very positive "Aha" moment. It was nothing new, nothing I had not been aware of before, but it struck me profoundly. "Yes it is!" I thought to myself. "We can never plumb its depths and in that it is a glorious mystery." For me it brought a new depth to the experience, it opened up new opportunities for thought and exploration, and I am impacted even as I write these words for consideration.

Discussion Questions for Scenario 2

1. Does the Lord's Supper strike you as a mystery?
2. How do you personally define a mystery?
3. Does it bother you when you can't get your mind around something?
4. Would you want to be involved in the Lord's Supper as a practice if you *could* understand it? If it wasn't a mystery?
5. Month after month we experience the Lord 's Supper in many different moods and temperaments. What are some of the differences in your experiences over the months? What is there in the service that creates or allows these differences? What is there in you that creates or allows these differences?

Lord's Supper Scenario 3

Since my retirement from pastoral ministry we have been attending a rather large church with about five hundred in worship on Sunday morning. It is the tradition of that church for individuals to go forward for the Lord's Supper. An individual can kneel at the communion rail and take the elements, a traditional cube of bread and a cup of grape juice; the server is one of the pastors, one of the ordained ministers in the congregation, or one of the lay ministers. Or, one can go forward and remain standing, taking the elements by breaking a piece of bread from a loaf held by a server, and dipping it into a cup of grape juice held by another server from the clergy / lay ministry group.

Looking back over my entire life, other than at informal youth retreats or at large gatherings in convention centers, I have never experienced the Lord's Supper other than it being served by diaconate to people sitting in pews, and so when we were there for the first time in this new setting I found the movement and style a bit disconcerting. I certainly was prepared not to like it, and I approached it with a critical, and probably defensive, eye. To my delight, however, I found it not only to be enjoyable, but very moving in different ways. As we sat and waited to go forward, I was moved by the image of families coming together and involving themselves. The tradition is of quietness, so there is no talking, no acknowledging of other people; one's focus is on the table and participating in it. I also found it special to kneel as I received the bread and cup, and I used that time to say a special prayer for my family, remembering each of them by name. Returning to my seat, there was time to reflect, to watch, to experience, to sing along with the hymns that were being played. In the end it was much more than I thought it would or could be.

Discussion Questions for Scenario 3

1. Over the years, how many different ways have you taken Communion?
2. Has one been "better" for you than others? If so why? How?
3. What do you do while Communion is being served? Does it become a holy moment for you? Or do you make out your grocery list? Or plan for the week ahead?
4. Does the level of your participation and awareness affect what you take away from it?
5. Does Jesus meet with you "where two or three are gathered?"
6. What is it that makes such a meeting happen—that makes it "work" for you?

Commentary on Scenario 3

One of the editors reviewing this manuscript penned in the margin a very interesting question: "Is communion an individual or a communal act?"

Thinking about it my immediate response was "Yes!" I meant this to mean that, "yes, it is individual" and "yes, it is communal." However, I know that to be simplistic, and I want to dig a little deeper.

I have always begun with the words of Jesus in Matthew 18:20: "For where two or three are gathered in my name, I am there among them." To my way of thinking, the gathered Church has always been a platform for worship because of that promise of Jesus to be with us; to be sure we experience him individually many times and that nurtures the relationship. But the corporate aspect of worship is something to which we are called to participate, and it brings a dimension that binds us together "with cords that cannot be broken."[12] As I sit in my pew on communion Sunday, before I go forward, and after I return, I see children, young people, couples holding hands, families, fathers and mothers with their arms embracing sons and daughter, elderly folk, and I am aware that I am very much a part of a larger group which we call Church. It hits me powerfully, and I think of those cords that bind us together.

At the same time when I kneel, I feel alone in the presence of my Lord, and my mind and heart reach out, sometimes with thanks, sometimes with a petition, always with an image of my family as I hold them to God's presence asking God to bless each one of them.

So for me Communion is both individual and corporate, both of them equally powerful in my worship experience. What is it for you?

Lord's Supper Scenario 4

You are delighted when a middle-aged couple new to the community begins to attend your church on a regular basis. They become regular in their involvement and, to your delight, ask for volunteer opportunities where they might be of service to the congregation. It may be just a coincidence, but at the same time the volunteer who prepares

---

[12] This is a line from an old hymn: "Bind us together, Lord; / Bind us together, Lord, / With cords that cannot be broken."

the communion elements each month has to resign for personal reasons. The woman says that she would be glad to pick up the responsibility, and has begun to do the preparation each month with faithfulness and competency. A number of months pass and you are extremely pleased with her commitment.

Then one day you receive a telephone call. A rumor has emerged, and the caller is sure that you would want to be aware of it. The rumor is that this couple is living together without benefit of marriage. When you ask them about it they acknowledge the rumor to be true; they believe that they have a commitment to each other, but they have not "legalized" that commitment through a formal marriage ceremony.

You are unsure as to what you should do. You believe that you live and work with a congregation of sinners, and one sin is no better or worse than any other sin. You argue with yourself that the woman's work is menial and behind the scenes and it shouldn't make any difference.

While your congregation says nothing in opposition to you, their feelings are quite evident when, on the next communion Sunday as the communion gathering hymn is sung, most of the congregation quietly leaves the sanctuary. You are later told that under no circumstances will they accept communion elements that have been prepared by "sinful hands."

Discussion Questions for Scenario 4

1. What are you thinking as you read this story?
2. If "sinful hands" cannot prepare communion elements, then who is there in the congregation who can prepare them? Who is without sin?
3. Is this a good time for the exercise of church discipline? How do we decide when church discipline should be used? What categories of sin demand it?
4. Are there categories of sin? Are there hierarchies of sin? Who determines the hierarchy if such exists?
5. How would you handle this situation? What steps would you take? Towards what end would you work?
6. Is there a principle at work here? What might it be? Is it possible that there might be conflicting principles?

7. Is it possible for a congregation to be wrong? How, if this is so, do you work with them?
8. Can a congregation immersed in blindness be led out of it?
9. What does forgiveness have to do with all of this?
10. Where is the Soul Freedom Principle at work here?
11. Where is the Biblical Authority Principle at work here?
12. Are they in tension with each other? Does one preempt the other? If so, which one and why?

Commentary on Scenario 4

As I write this scenario I am reminded of the preacher who asked during a sermon a rhetorical question: "Is there any one here this morning who is without sin, perfect in every way?" You can imagine the preacher's surprise when a man stood up. "Charlie," the minister asked, "are you claiming to be perfect?" "No," Charlie responded, "but I thought I would stand in for my wife's first husband."

This story about the couple living together, being new in the community, and the woman preparing the communion elements, is a true story. I heard it from a friend of mine at the February 2010 Minister's Colloquium sponsored by the Ministers and Missionaries Benefit Board of the American Baptist Churches, for ministers of the larger American Baptist Churches. He knew firsthand of the experience through an individual who was a member in the church in which this story took place. It is related pretty much as he told it to me, though it is impossible for me to convey the incredulity in his voice.

7

The Priesthood of the Individual Believer

When I hear the word "priest" I think of office and of position. I think of the individual who facilitates the Eucharistic transformation of wafer and wine into the actual body and blood of Jesus Christ. I think of the individual who sits in the confessional hearing individual confessions, who is the representative of God and thus able to declare the forgiveness of sins. I sense with this individual an aura of the holy and of the mysterious.

I am conditioned by my heritage. I was born in New England amongst the Irish Catholics; all of my life I heard family and friends speak of their church and their faith. My father was raised a Roman Catholic; one of his brothers and two of his sisters remained of that faith, and I would often hear them speak with awe about this one whom they respected so highly, in fact whom they revered. He had God in him in a very special way!

Mystery! Mysterious! Many were the afternoons that I sat in a darkened church with candles burning brightly, small pinpoints of light that danced with the movement of air and that cast shadows across the wall and the statues that lined it. This indeed, was nothing like my church, but I would loyally sit and wait while John, my best friend, went to confession. When he came out of the confessional he had some instructions from the priest, what he needed to do as an act of penance for his sins. When finished he would be absolved and only then would we hoist up our books and begin the mile-plus walk home. I have to make a personal confession here; there were many days when I wished that getting rid of my sins, being absolved of them, could be as easy as that. I know I simplify what the Church would say was very complex; I only know that it seemed simple to me, it felt that way to me.

The idea of the priest, or holy one, or shaman, is inherent in every culture since the dawn of humanity. This is clear out of the study and writings of Carl Jung and Joseph Campbell, which demonstrate that some form of religious expression is found in even the most primitive societies. The need for a priest seems to emerge out of the deepest regions of the human psyche as we seek to cope with the vicissitudes of life and reconcile what appears to us to be evil with that eternal creative force that we identify as God. Someone was needed to bridge the gap between the sacred and the profane.

For us as Baptists, however, specifically as a people of the Bible, our idea of the priest was born in the Old Testament. The priesthood was explicit in the covenant that God established with Israel. God agreed to be the God of the descendants of Abraham as they lived in the land that God was to give to them. The descendants of Abraham agreed that they would be faithful in the living out of their lives according to the precepts of this God who had called them, who would guide them, and who would be present in the course of their lives and relationships.

In this, God clearly stated that the being of God was jealous in nature, and this jealousy would allow no other gods to be placed "before me" (Ex 20:3). The Ten Commandments and the Mosaic Code came out of this covenant. With it, Israel agreed that as God's chosen people they would adopt these commandments and this code; this meant that they would lead lives in keeping with the code and the commandments. Furthermore, it meant that they would honor the rituals of sacrifice and worship that would keep the lines of holiness and communication open.

Historically, as Israel came out of Egypt and wandered forty years in the wilderness, as Moses implemented at God's direction the temple and worship within that temple, as the Ark of the Covenant became the "seat of God" in their midst, the Levites were designated to serve the Ark and to take responsibility for moving and sustaining the sanctuary. Out of this, it became the prerogative of the Levites to expound on the Mosaic Law as it developed, to interpret what it meant in varying circumstances, and to perform the ritual sacrifices at the altar, as they were needed.[1]

Practically, what this meant was that when the people moved away from the commitment that they had made, it was the priest who called them back and who in offering their sacrifice channeled the forgiveness of the God whom they had wronged. The function of the individual or the corporate priesthood was to assure, to maintain, and to reestablish

---

[1] Melvin D. Rehm, "Levites and Priests," *The Anchor Bible Dictionary*, ed. David Noel Freedman (New York: Doubleday, 1992) 305.

the rightness with God of the chosen people, individually and collectively, of God. An individual could certainly pray to God—remember the story of Hannah in the temple praying to God for a child (1 Sam 1:9–11)? It was the priest who intermediated in the offering of the sacrifice. Only a priest could dispense forgiveness and grace through the act of sacrifice, and it was only through sacrifice of animal, of grain, of substance, that forgiveness and grace could be received. The priest took your words of confession to God, your avowals of repentance and love, and then brought God's word of pardon back to you. Only the priest had the sight to see, and the ears to hear on another's behalf, the mind and the will of God.

There was separation here; God was in heaven; humanity was on earth, and the priesthood stood between the two, being the bridge, the only means of communication.

In the concept of the priesthood there was a priest who stood above all other priests, and he was designated as the high priest (Hebrews 7 and 8). He was the priest to the nation. He and he alone could approach God in the Holy of Holies, that inner sanctuary of the temple that held the Ark of the Covenant and which was the seat, the dwelling place of God. Only he could part the veil which brought him into the very presence of God. Only he could make the sacrifice on behalf of the nation on the Day of Atonement. He bore on the ephod, the breastplate that he wore, the names of the twelve tribes;[2] so it was that when he approached God, he did so on behalf of the entire people. He was an intercessor on behalf of the people of the nation, the called out people of God.

In the New Testament this concept of the priest was radically changed. It was moved from the institution of the temple and the tribe and transferred to the individual believer. Everyone called of God, everyone with a personal commitment to Jesus Christ, is a priest. We are priests because we are a part of the covenant of redemption offered to us by God through Jesus Christ. We are made priests by means of the redemptive work of Jesus Christ on the cross. The Revelation of John clearly says, "To him who loves us and freed us from our sins by his blood, and made us to be a kingdom, priests serving his God and Father, to him be glory and dominion forever and ever. Amen" (1:5b–6).

---

[2] See Exodus 28 on the construction of the ephod.

This concept of the Priesthood of the Individual Believer is spelled out even more clearly in 1 Peter 2:4–10. In verse 2:5 Peter says: "like living stones let yourselves be built into a spiritual house, to be a holy priesthood, to offer spiritual sacrifices acceptable to God through Jesus Christ." In verse 2:9 Peter goes on to say: "But you are a chosen race, a royal priesthood, a holy nation, God's own people, in order that you may proclaim the mighty acts of him who called you out of darkness into his marvelous light." Here Peter is drawing on the language of the Sinai covenant; we must acknowledge the connectedness between this Christian community that is emerging out of Judaism, and its roots in the Jewish/Hebrew Bible. (Please note here that in the second portion of verse nine there is a practical function to be lived out in the life of the priest or the believer; we will have more on this, but hold the thought.)

What does Peter mean? He is speaking here of the Church, the Church built of living stones, the Church built with the life of every person who lives or who ever lived who expressed their faith in Jesus Christ as Savior and Lord. He is making it very clear that every believer is a priest in that Church, and that every believer as such has equal access to God. We know from our own study of the Bible that the symbol of this accessibility took place when, on the cross, Jesus gave up his spirit. In that moment, the veil of the temple, that which separated the Holy of Holies from the Holy Place—that which was a symbol of separateness and exclusiveness—was rent, split asunder (Mk 15:37–38). This became the symbol of access, indicating that every believer, as priest, might now enter directly into the presence of God. We need neither mediators to bring our needs to God's attention nor dispensers of divine favor to bring God's grace to us. God is as near to us as our hearts for indeed it is there where God dwells. God speaks clearly to us through that still small voice of conscience, and through the love of God's people. We are, in words of Paul, heirs, the children of God, adopted of God with all of the rights and privileges of those who might be natural born. We have been claimed. We belong to God (Rom 8:15–17).

Historical Development

Since the time of the early Church there evolved a very strong priesthood, considered to have apostolic succession back to Peter, the first (in the Church's eyes) leader or "pope" of the Church. This meant that the priest was an inheritor of the keys to the kingdom, keys that could access or deny entrance to heaven. Only the priest could forgive sin, and the priest literally held in his hands the soul's consignment to heaven or to the burning fires of hell.[3]

Martin Luther was amongst the first to challenge this concept of the priesthood as he sought to dialogue with his own Church over Church beliefs and practices that he found incompatible with Scripture. In one of these challenges he said "Christ has made it possible for us ... to be ... his fellow priests."[4]

Luther was a part of a chorus beginning to swell, and his idea of this biblical model of the priesthood recaptured was picked up on by the two leaders who formed the first Baptist church in Amsterdam in 1609: John Smyth and Thomas Helwys.[5] John Smyth saw the church as "a 'kingly priesthood' and that the saints (or Christians) are 'kings and priests.'"[6] Helwys went on to say of King James I, "[The king] hath no power over ye immortall soules of his subjects, to make lawes and ordinances for them, and to set spirituall Lords over them."[7]

Creeds and Confessions of Faith

As Baptists we are not creedal; we are, however, confessional. There is a difference. In 1969, Judson Press published a book edited by W.L. Lumpkin titled, *Baptist Confessions of Faith*. For me it turned out to be a book I came to treasure, and over forty years of ministry I have often taken it down from the bookshelf in preparation for a class or a sermon

[3] To illustrate this idea more fully, see chapter two and the narrative story of John.

[4] Martin Luther, *Three Treatises* (Philadelphia: Fortress Press, 1960) 290.

[5] I want to acknowledge that for the prior thought on Martin Luther, and this information on John Smyth and Thomas Helwys, I am indebted to Google search finding an article "The Priesthood of All Believers" by Carolyn D. Blevins. This article is one of nine pamphlets in a series, "The Baptist Style for a New Century," jointly published by the Baptist History and Heritage Society and the William H. Whitsitt Baptist Heritage Society.

[6] Ibid., 4.

[7] Thomas Helwys, "A Short Declaration of the Mystery of Iniquity," in *Baptist Ways, A History*, by Bill J. Leonard (Valley Forge PA: Judson Press, 2003) 26.

or for a special presentation or to remind myself that we have a wonderful heritage that still speaks to and for us in incredible ways. Beginning with Balthasar Hubmaier's *Eighteen Dissertations* in 1524, Lumpkin takes the reader through confessions that represent the emerging Reformation before moving on to Early English Baptist Associational Confessions to English Baptist General Confessions, to American Baptist Confessions, and to Confessions of Other Nationalities. None of these confessions should be confused with a creed.

Creeds came out of the historical development of the Church, and their sources many times came from a Council convened to come to conclusions about differing theological dogma. Creeds became statements of theological belief; they were definitive, official documents defining the position of the Church and often read as a part of the Church liturgy. I see a creed as much more authoritative, speaking absolutely for the Church. Some well-known creeds include the Apostles' Creed, the Nicene Creed, and the Athanasian Creed.

While Baptists would agree theologically with many of the creeds as they are, we do not like to be so definitive, for Soul Freedom and the Priesthood of the Believer suggests that at some time new truth might be revealed to us. I see a strong difference in that confessions are simply a way of saying "as we covenant together this is something that we believe—this is where we are at the moment." Many Baptist confessions have a disclaimer, such as that found in the London Confession of Faith from 1644: "Also we confesse that we know but in part, and that we are ignorant of many things which we desire and seek to know: and if any shall doe us that friendly part to shew us from the word of God that we see not, we shall have cause to be thankfull to God and them."[8]

Speaking here on the Priesthood of the Individual Believer, it is important to note that this theme from the London Confession runs through each of these confessions, and well it should, for it is an important part of the fabric of which we are woven.

---

[8] William L. Lumpkin, *Baptist Confessions of Faith* (Valley Forge PA: Judson Press, 1969) 149.

The Priesthood of the Individual Believer and Soul Freedom

Soul Freedom and the Priesthood of the Individual Believer are closely related, for individual priesthood springs out of the idea of Soul Freedom. God has given us an intellect with which to think, an intuitive sense to feel and draw in information, and a soul that bears the imprint of the image of God within us. With this we are given the responsibility for developing and nurturing our faith. It is as priests that we do this due diligence in seeking God's will for our lives and the communities in which we live. It is also as priests that we live out those conclusions as to who God wants us to be and what God wants us to do. We are chosen not for special privilege, but rather for special responsibility. Hopefully this was clear in the opening chapter on Soul Freedom.

Implications and Responsibilities of the Priesthood of the Individual Believer

If the redemptive work of Christ makes the believer into a Priesthood, if we as the people of God born in faith are equal before God, if our personal encounter with Jesus Christ brings us into a covenantal relationship as the family of God, then there are implications in all of this for our lives and responsibilities as to the way that we live them.

First we understand that we all have equal access to the Scriptures and to all of the means through which we believe the grace of God is bestowed upon the people of God. This we know to be the source, the bedrock, of our strength and our encouragement. The Holy Spirit speaks to each of us individually when we earnestly approach God's throne of grace, which we do through prayer, study and reflection. We do know the disastrous consequences to our faith journey and practice if we do not take the time to listen to that inner voice; or to study the Word and the interpreters of the Word; or to learn its meaning and to apply it to our lives; or to attempt to grow closer to God and to each other; and to lead better lives. The Bible is like our roadmap, and we know what can happen when we go on a trip and leave the map in the glove compartment or fail to turn on the GPS. Take a wrong turn, ignore all of the warning signs, and our trip to Florida could end up in Alabama. It is inconceivable that we don't read and pray more when we sincerely believe that this is one of the primary ways in which God communicates with us.

Beyond this, we must explore the other ways in which God might be revealed to us. With this we must include prayer, meditation, fellowship with other believers, and/or service and mission on behalf of others.

Second, if we claim the Priesthood of All Believers, then it is clear that there are no divisions, that there can be no divisions among the people of God. We are equal before God, all dressed in the same garments of righteousness and grace. Individually, no one is better than any other; individually, no one is more important than any other. In fact many times, to our consternation and distress, our supposed rankings are reversed—one of those great reversals in the kingdom of God (of which there are many) and in God's sight the first shall be last and the last shall be first. Humility trumps power and authority every time! Yes, there are offices; some are called to be pastors, some teachers, and some apostles. But these are divisions not of importance but of function and responsibility. Jesus set the pattern for this; all were the same in his sight, including the thief on the cross, the children, the foreigner, the prostitute, the tax collector, and the sheep that was lost. The practical qualities of James 2 is one of many good New Testament examples as to how the early followers of Jesus were obsessed with this democratic complex. If we believe that there is no one, no thing that stands between God and us, the next declaration must be that there are no, or rather there shouldn't be any, divisions to separate us as the people of God

Third, a part of the privilege and responsibility of the priest is to offer sacrifices. Paul spoke of the offering of our bodies, indeed our very lives, as a sacrifice to God (Rom 12:1–2). I interpret this to mean that everything we are and everything we have is on the altar before God—a recognition that it belongs to God and not to us.[9]

Fourth, a significant part of this priestly responsibility is proclamation. In every context, in every way possible, either verbal or in deed and action, we are to speak the good news of Gospel. As believers we interpret this to mean: "The Spirit of the Lord is upon *me*, because he

---

[9] Preachers, I hope that you will recognize here the seeds of a stewardship sermon!

has anointed *me* to bring good news to the poor. He has sent *me* to proclaim release to the captives and recovery of sight to the blind, to let the oppressed go free, to proclaim the year of the Lord's favor" (Lk 4:18–19). So often we limit proclamation to the clergy or about evangelism, but the gospel is far richer than that, and it is appointed to be the calling of each believer. This leads us to our next privilege and responsibility as priests.

Fifth, social justice is a part of this proclamation, healing the injustices of poverty, of hunger, touching the pain and the hurt of the world with the healing balm of God's grace. The word of the priests and the prophets was that "justice roll down like waters and righteousness like an ever flowing stream" (Am 5:24). The word of Jesus was to feed the hungry, clothe the naked, visit those who are sick and in prison (Mt 25). In modern parlance, this is going beyond "talking the talk" and "walking the walk," and is the talk and walk of each priestly follower.

Sixth, yet another function of being a priest is intercession. This means that we are to pray on behalf of others, to intercede before God for others and for the world. To bring others, with their needs, hopes, aspirations, sorrows, pain, and illness, into the presence of God is both a responsibility and a privilege. Fred Craddock speaks of being in a prayer meeting at the beginning of the Gulf War, where a young man prayed that, "God be with the women and the children in Iraq who would be hurt and killed in the war." Following the meeting, an older man approached and asked the young man, "Are you on Saddam's side?" To the reply "No, sir," he said "Well, you're praying for the wrong people."[10] We declare "Absolutely not!" to that statement; more than anything else, that young man was on the right track. It is the love and compassion that we cultivate through the disciplined life which enables us, encourages us, if not demands of us, to break down all barriers and to bring all needs before the presence of God.

These are things that we take for granted, the ability, for example, to stop what we are doing and offer a prayer, bringing ourselves directly into the presence of God. I have found that we need to cultivate, in fact we need to deeply desire this role of priest in order to enable us to

[10] Mike Graves, and Richard F. Ward, ed. *Craddock Stories* (Louisville KY: Chalice Press, 2001) 130.

function as priest. It is only thus that we can actually do the kinds of priestly actions which we are called to live out in our lives. But we also need the discipline and the caring heart that moves us out of ourselves to stand before God on behalf of others.

Seventh, speaking here on our privilege and responsibility as priests, we cannot omit the matter of worship. Worship is foundational to who we are, joining together as the people of God in community. Here we open our hearts and minds to God in word, praise, prayer, and adoration.

My challenge, both personally and to my readers, is to realize who we are in our calling and in our conviction of faith. This means accepting the awesome responsibility and privilege we have in being God's priests at work in the world. We do this that we might grow in faith and that the world might know God's word in Jesus Christ, because we have brought it to them through intercession and ministry.

The Priesthood of the Believer and Ordination

In the historic Church, with its hierarchy of leadership, the office of the priest was definitely one of authority, and a wide gap existed between that power and the laity. With its doctrine of the Priesthood of the Individual Believer, the Reformation leveled the playing field. If we are all priests and as priests have equal access to God without the need of an intermediator, it fair to ask about the justification for an ordained ministry.

Such a question begins with the idea of spiritual gifts as outlined by the Apostle Paul (Rom 12:3–8, 1 Cor 12–14, Eph 4:7–3). Paul said that these gifts were God-given, were different within each individual, and were intended for the glory of God in the mission and ministry of the Church. Each of us is called by God to be diligent and faithful in the exercise of these gifts given to us so freely.

Ordination is a special recognition by the Church of an individual who gives evidence of a call to ministry, who demonstrates the specific gifts for ministry, and who then is set aside as a servant to the Church. These gifts might include service, preaching, leadership, and compassion, to name a few. The pastoral office carries no extra status; it is subservient to the will of the congregation. Authority continues to rest with the congregation.

"Ordination for Baptists is a service of thanksgiving for God's love revealed in the minister's calling, a service of petition for God's continued blessing upon the one called, and a service of submission to God's authority revealed in the gifted one set aside for ministry."[11]

Topics for Discussion

Priesthood of the Individual Believer Scenario 1

It is a quiet day in your office, and you are enjoying some study time. A rap on your office door distracts you, and you look up to see a young woman asking you if you have a few minutes to spare. You invite her in to sit down, and your mind is racing to try and place her, but it doesn't work, and you are relieved when she apologizes for coming in on a whim as she was driving by and has no relationship to your church at all. You ask for her story and she begins to tell you what is bothering her, and what has brought her in. In her monologue there are several references to "father" and "priest" and you gain some understanding that her religious background is something other than Baptist. You would suspect Episcopalian or Roman Catholic, but you do not want to interrupt her story to ask. In her unfolding story it is very clear that she is carrying a heavy burden of guilt; there is something that she has done that violates and puts at jeopardy her relationship with God, and she wants to know if you can help her make that right. As she drove by there was something about the church building that seemed to invite her in. As she finishes her story she looks directly into your eyes and asked if you would pray for her. Would you pray that God would forgive her for what she had done? Would you give her God's blessing? You agree, and you do that, and as she walks from your office you realize that there is a bounce in her step that was not there when she came in—she is leaving released from her burden. You think to yourself, "I wish it were that easy!" Then you begin to think about what happened, and you wonder if you should have done things differently.

---

[11] William Loyd Allen, "The Meaning of Ordination," The Baptist History and Heritage Society. http://www.baptisthistory.org/bhhs/21stcentury/ordination.html

Discussion Questions for Scenario 1

1. What is your initial reaction to this story as you read it?
2. Why do you think she didn't just offer a prayer for herself?
3. Why do you thing she had the feeling that she needed you to pray for her? Where did that come from?
4. What do you think she is suggesting about her image of the pastoral office?
5. With her suspected liturgical background, you realize that she has just confessed her sins to you and you have absolved them, at least in her eyes. Do you agree? If you agree how do you feel about that? Do you want to go back and undo the experience?
6. Should you have given her a lecture on the difference between a Roman Catholic priest and a Baptist pastor?
7. Do you think that such nuances would have been lost on her? Or would it have been a "eureka" moment?
8. What could/should you have told her about the Priesthood of the Individual Believer?
9. Would that have been an appropriate moment for a didactic lecture?
10. Should you refuse her request to pray for her, telling her that her own prayer is sufficient for forgiveness?
11. To what degree does your agreeing to pray for her play into her priestly image and undo all that you are trying to tell or teach her?
12. Do you ever wonder if sometimes those of us who are pastors actually do believe in the deepest parts of our beings that, because we have been chosen by God, we do, in fact, have access beyond the ordinary?

Commentary on Scenario 1

This story happened exactly as I have written it. My church at that time was First Baptist Church of Malden, Massachusetts. Malden was a suburb of Boston, right on the Orange Line (public subway transit) and less than fifteen minutes from downtown Boston. Malden had about sixty thousand residents, and was home to several very large Roman Catholic parishes. First Baptist Church stood at the corner of Main and Salem streets, close to downtown and one of the busier intersections in the city.

Jesus made forgiveness easy. Think of Mark 11:24 (So I tell you, whatever you ask for in prayer, believe that you have received it, and it will be yours) and Luke 11:9 (So I say to you, Ask, and it will be given you; search, and you will find; knock, and the door will be opened for you). The woman who visited that day believed this. She asked, she received, and it appeared to me that she left free of the burden with which she had entered my office.

I made the comment in the text that "I wish it were that easy." It may be that some personality types struggle more with our angst than others. It may be that we want to have a process that demands retribution, with some kind of a penalty being paid. The stories of the Bible recount people with these very same issues; they were astounded when a loving father forgave a prodigal son without question (Lk 15:11–32), when vineyard workers were paid the same amount even though they had worked different numbers of hours (Mt 20:1–16). Grace without penalty continues to be a struggle for some of us.

It is, perhaps, worth another question. What do you think about forgiveness? Grace? Penalty? Retribution?

Priesthood of the Individual Believer Scenario 2

You are about to head out of town the next morning when you receive a call from one of your most active members. Her husband will be going into the hospital in the morning for what could be very serious surgery, and the family would like you to come and have prayer with them. You explain your situation and the necessity for your trip, and you offer to join them in their home that evening for prayer. They are somewhat disappointed that you will not be there in the morning, but you tell them that you will have one of the deacons or Stephen Ministers[12] available to them. Later on you begin to hear rumblings on the grapevine and it is obvious that they have been sharing their displeasure with their friends. Yes, they did appreciate your evening visit. Individually, however, and as a family, they really needed prayer

---

[12] Stephen Ministry is a national program offering training in congregational care. It offers participants an opportunity to work with those who are in need of a caregiver, and it encourages accountability so that checks and balances are in place. When I took Stephen Ministry training in the mid-eighties, it was a two-week commitment to become a Stephen Ministry Leader.

that morning as they surgery was imminent. Their collective anxiety was especially high. For these reasons, they did not appreciate that instead of coming yourself, even though it would have meant changing your plans, you had sent the "second string." Why, those who came (Stephen Ministers) weren't even ordained ministers!

Discussion Questions for Scenario 2

1. What is your initial reaction as you read this story?
2. Do you feel that what she is asking, that you change your plans, is an unrealistic expectation? How do you deal with those kinds of unrealistic expectations? Are they in fact unreasonable?
3. How do you address this particular issue?
4. Would it help to tell them that you think them to be selfish, demanding, and needy?
5. Would you confront them with the "gossip" they are spreading in the church, and the damage that the tongue can do to the church's wellbeing?
6. What does the principle of the Priesthood of the Individual believer mean in this situation?
7. How do you talk to the people of your church about the principle of the Priesthood of the Individual Believer? Are pastoral prayers any more efficacious than those of a deacon or Stephen Minister?
8. What do they say when you tell them that, as pastor, you have agreed to provide them with pastoral ministry in life's difficult situations, but you did not agree that it would always be you doing the ministry.
9. When pastors are put on pedestals and deemed to be the only ones who can "really" meet certain pastoral needs, is there any truth in the observation that we encourage this?
10. Is there any truth in the observation that we foster and nurture it by our own activities and declarations?

Priesthood of the Individual Believer Scenario 3

You have been extremely busy and, as a result, your spiritual disciplines have been sadly lacking. It has been a few weeks since you have really taken the time to pray, to read the Scripture, to sit and think about spiritual matters, to sit and listen for the voice of the Holy Spirit to speak to you. You feel coldness and darkness, you feel like you are running on empty, and then one day you realize that you do not feel very priestly any more.

Discussion Questions for Scenario 3

1. Does this description resonate with you?
2. Are ministers, because of their high calling, immune to such depressions?
3. What does it mean to dispel darkness and coldness?
4. Are there requirements to being a priest?
5. Do we always have to be "up" to do good priestly and pastoral work?
6. How do we function when the "dark night of the soul" is upon us?
7. What are the foundations of priestly prayer and priestly living? What are the things that we need to do to take care of ourselves spiritually?
8. What does it mean to you when, in Peter's letter, he clearly says that we are priests? Individually? With complete access to God? To do holy work?
9. What is holy work to you?

Priesthood of the Individual Believer Scenario 4

As you are preaching a sermon on the principle of the Priesthood of the Individual Believer, you bring to the congregation a strong challenge. If they are serious about their Christian faith, they will go beyond tithing and prayer and spiritual disciplines. Indeed, if they are deeply into the Spirit and into intercession as called for in Scripture, they will go out and work in the food pantry, or they will go out and build a Habitat House, or they will also go out and work in a shelter for battered women.

Discussion Questions for Scenario 4

1. What are the social justice implications of living out the Priesthood of the Individual Believer?
2. What does it mean to be a priest in terms of social justice?

3. Martin Luther King, Jr., once spoke of "standing up for justice." What do you think that he meant? What does this mean personally to you?
4. What are five areas in your local community where God would want you doing social justice in your work and responsibility as a priest?
5. What do priests do when they are practicing social justice?
6. Is this something radically different from other demands on our time?
7. Is it possible that working in the arena of social justice could be prophetic?

Priesthood of the Individual Believer Scenario 5
(Also: Soul Freedom, Biblical Authority)

A group of people active within the life of your church approaches you with a request to meet with the governing body of the church. They declare their intention to propose that the church withdraw its affiliation with the denomination to which you belong. They cite many of the controversial stands that the denomination has made in its policy statements, stands that do not represent the theology of your church. They also cite the decline in denominationalism, with denominational loyalty very low on the preference level of those seeking a new church.

Discussion Questions for Scenario 5

1. As a church leader, what are the issues that would move you to consider fracturing your historic relationship with your denomination?
2. What are the requirements of denominational community? What are the responsibilities of denominational community?
3. In this instance what do you sense is behind the thinking of those who have come to see you? Are these any different from the issues you annunciated in the first question to this scenario?
4. Are there questions of Biblical Authority here? If so, what are they?
5. How do Biblical Authority and the Priesthood of the Individual Believer intersect in this scenario?

6. How does Soul Freedom interact here with both Biblical Authority and the Priesthood of the Individual Believer? Why can't we live together within our differences?
7. Are there certain issues that promote schism as opposed to other issues? If so, why is it we can be tolerable with one issue and intolerable with another?
8. Does denominational loyalty have to be blind?
9. What does it mean to be prophetic within denominational life?
10. Is denominational loyalty everlasting? Or are there appropriate times for schism?
11. On the other hand, what do schisms say to the world about the Church?
12. Is this act of removal from the denomination taking personal priesthood too far?
13. Would you allow the group who approached you to make such a presentation to the church leadership? If so, what would you say when asked to speak to the issue?
14. If the church withdrew from the denomination, how would that affect your tenure as minister or as a church leader?

Priesthood of the Individual Believer Scenario 6
(Also: Soul Freedom, Biblical Authority)

You are approached by the chairman of your board of trustees. He tells you that he is active in the local Masonic Lodge and that the members of the Lodge would like to attend church as a group on a not too distant Sunday. You ask him what this involves. He tells you that it would mean marching in to reserved seating during the opening hymn, and that they would be wearing full Masonic regalia including formal tuxedos, Masonic aprons and badges, Commandery regalia including hats, which are versions of old naval hats complete with feathers and plumes, with swords at their side.

Discussion Questions for Scenario 6

1. What are you thinking as you sit and listen?
2. Do you tell him that it is the silliest thing that you have ever heard?

3. Do you give him a lecture about secret societies? What do you believe about secret societies? Is it acceptable for Christians to join secret societies?
4. Do you give him a lecture about wearing hats and weapons in church?
5. What does this have to do with the Priesthood of the Individual Believer?
6. What does this have to do with the intersection of Priesthood and Soul Freedom?
7. What does this have to do with Priesthood and Biblical Authority?
8. How do the multiple Baptist Principles interact here?
9. Many masons see a strong relationship between their Masonic beliefs and their Christian faiths, for after all, Masonry is built on stories and principles of the Bible. How do you interpret and/or understand this overlap?
10. How do you respond to this request? Do you make a wholehearted offer or do you place conditions and restrictions?
11. What action do you suggest and why?
12. What are the political ramifications within the life of the church of your decision?
13. Would it make a difference if the person making the request were your spouse? The moderator of your church? The chair of the Search Committee that made the pastoral call recommendation? Your best friend in the congregation? One of your children? Your wealthiest member who is a tither? A friend from Rotary Club?

Commentary on Scenario 6

This was an experience I had while pastor of First Baptist Church of Malden, Massachusetts. Through the prodding of an active church member, I had agreed to join the local Rotary Club, and it was one of the men from Rotary who made the request to me. It just so happened that he was the local plumber who did all of our church work and who, on several occasions, had come out after hours or on the weekend to fix something at the parsonage. I do not have problems with the Masons; I grew up with my grandfather and uncle very active members, and in high school I had been a member of the DeMolay, a Masonic program for young men. I did have a bit of a problem with the hats and swords, but learned that they were part of the regalia, and in the end found that they removed their hats as they sat down and that the swords were merely ceremonial.

On that particular Sunday, approximately one hundred Masons marched down the center aisle during the opening hymn and took their places in the first rows of the church—the ones that are never filled. I chose to preach that morning on the story of Solomon and the temple, a topic that resonated with them, and they were very attentive during the sermon and very complimentary as they went out.

In the end there were no negatives to the experience. There were however, a significant number of positives. First of all, it helped boost the attendance for the day—always a good move. Second, it was good to have some people in the front rows in a sanctuary that seated 700 and a regular congregation that averaged about 240. Third, it was absolutely incredible to have people sitting close enough to the pulpit so that I actually could see the whites of their eyes. Was it only my opinion that my preaching was much better that day? Fourth, a number of the Masons were members of the Rotary Club, and later on, over several years, the club through its community programs allocated significant funding to help me with some wilderness camping trips that we were sponsoring for the youth of the church and the community. Fifth, many of those men, especially from the Rotary, invited me to share in some pastoral responsibilities in their lives, which I considered to be a great ministerial opportunity.

It turned out to be a very simple, magnanimous gesture, and the dividends were far greater than I could have imagined.

Priesthood of the Individual Believer Scenario 7

It is a Friday evening, and your son/daughter is graduating from high school. Because of his/her academic achievement he/she will be recognized and be gifted with one of the speaking topics that form the ceremony. Your son/daughter and spouse have left the house early; you will leave shortly to join them with the rest of the family. Just as you are going out of the door, the telephone rings. It is one of your most active church members calling to tell you that her husband had had (an accident/stroke/heart attack/emergency appendectomy) and it is very important to them that you get to the hospital immediately.

Discussion Questions for Scenario 7

1. Is the first thing you do to utter a mild cuss word (only to yourself, of course)?
2. Do you get upset with yourself and think, "I shouldn't have answered the telephone?"
3. While you breathe a sigh of anguish, do you realize that you have a call to pastoral ministry and a call to be the shepherd to the sheep?
4. Do you understand that this has happened before and that your family knows who is paying your salary and that the needs of others must come first?
5. Does it occur to you that your spouse and your daughter are sheep who are shepherds within your flock? Are their needs less important than those of someone in the hospital?
6. Does one situation trump the other? Or does one need trump the other because it is greater? If a need is greater, who determines that? You? Your spouse? Your son/daughter? The church member waiting for you at the hospital?
7. Is it possible that a member of the diaconate could be called to rush to the hospital for prayer?
8. Is it possible that a Stephen Minister could be sent to the hospital for prayer?
9. Is it possible that a hospital chaplain could be called for prayer?
10. Is it possible that someone other than you could utter a prayer in these circumstances that would be heard by God?
11. Being a priest herself, why don't you suggest that the wife say a prayer for her husband in her priestly role?
12. Would a woman minister handle this matter any differently than a male minister would? If not, why do you think that is true? If so, why do you think that is true?
13. What are the implications of this request all around?
14. Is it possible that what this individual is demanding is unreasonable?

15. Is it possible that this is not about ministry but about power and control? What do you think I mean by this question?
16. Would it matter if the woman calling were the chair of your church board?
17. Would it matter if her tithe were the largest church gift? A sizable portion of the budget?
18. What do you say to the wife? What action do you take?
19. Which is the better course, dealing with an irate parishioner, or an irate and hurt spouse and son/daughter?
20. Is there an alternative which meets everyone's needs and expectations?
21. Do you think that this question is age-sensitive—that younger ministers today are more aware and responsible to their families than those of us of a previous generation?
22. Do they have a better understanding of church and ministry?

Commentary on Scenario 7

Rationally this is a very easy situation to handle. You are a parent, and there are times when you simply have to put your family first. It seems to me that this would be one of them. This is especially true when we realize that there are a host of other solutions to meet the needs of ministry at the hospital, whereas there is only one solution for your spouse and son/daughter.

However, psychological studies tell us that many who enter the ministry score high on the "people pleaser" end of the personality scale; in other words, they want their actions to be pleasing to other people.

To those individuals for whom this scenario is a true dilemma, this is an agonizing situation, for it would mean antagonizing a very important church member, and quite frankly, for many in ministry it is easier to have your spouse and/or son/daughter upset than an important church member. Family loves us and they will get over it. That is not always true for active church members.

I remember someone telling me of how they had grown up in a parsonage, and every summer they would spend some time at a cottage or camp that was about a day's drive from home. They went on to say that they cannot remember a single summer in all their years of growing up that their father did not have to make the drive back at least once for some kind of pastoral "emergency." They simply got used to having vacations with their father absent for some of the time.

It is true that ordained ministers are called to be servants. It is true that legitimate pastoral needs of an emergency nature arise at the most inopportune times. It is also true that the church can be insatiable; it will take every thing we have to give, and it will not be enough. I can remember one of my seminary professors identifying the church as a "demanding mother who cannot be satisfied."[13]

But it is also very true that our spouses and our families need us too, and we need them as well. Because of this, there are times when we have to set limits. I believe this is true as much for ourselves as it is for the church.

I remember being called to the critical care unit at the hospital; a man had had a stroke and was near death. I went each day for several days to be with the family and to say a prayer in his presence, and I was called to be with the family when he died. The widow thanked me for my prayers and my care, and said that she would be calling me, that there was no one else in the entire world that they would allow to do the funeral other than me. I admit to being flattered. When the funeral director called, however, the funeral was scheduled at a time when I had a conflict that I could not break. I told him that, and suggested that if they would move it to the next day I would have no problem. He called me back to say that the widow wanted to "get it over with" and they would get someone else. This is how we learn lessons, and gain perspective! There were a lot of subsequent situations where I was much, much better at setting limits, doing pastoral ministry but also being responsible to myself and my own needs, and my family and their needs.

Priesthood of the Individual Believer Scenario 8

In early 2010, a federal judge responded favorably to a suit that asked the court to declare unconstitutional a movement to create a National Day of Prayer.

The suit was brought by the Freedom from Religion Foundation in Wisconsin. It cited that the creation of a day of prayer was a violation of

---

[13] To be fair, he also said that the church could be a "nurturing mother" as well, and that is true, but it is not germane to our argument here.

the rights of those who do not pray, and referenced the Establishment Clause in the Constitution. Interestingly the group found support from interfaith organizations who said that the conservative right had taken over the days of prayer with little inclusion of the wider faith community, from the Baptist Joint Committee for Religious liberty who suggested that "a National Day of Prayer was 'misguided,'"[14] and from Americans United for Separation of Church and State who said, "Congress has no business telling Americans when or how to pray."[15]

Proponents were incensed. One congressman said, "That's not what the Constitution says; that's what one unelected judge says the Constitution says."[16] The *Christian Century* article suggested lively debate in political circles, for "who wants to say we don't support prayer?"[17]

Discussion Questions for Scenario 8

1. Do you agree with the judge's decision? Why? Why not?
2. Is she correct in citing the Establishment Clause?
3. Do you feel that the quote of the congressman reflects general public opinion?
4. Would you give money to support the Baptist Joint Committee for Religious Liberty, and Americans United for Separation of Church and State? Are they out of touch with the values of most Americans? Are they defenders of freedoms and principles that we treasure?
5. What do you think are the separation of church and state issues at work here?

Separation of Church and State Scenario 9

In the spring of 2010, the Pentagon planned to hold an interfaith prayer service. They had invited as their speaker the Rev. Franklin Graham, founder of the world relief agency Samaritan's Purse.

There were some, however, who found his leadership controversial; they spoke of Graham's remarks made some years previously regarding

---

[14] "Appeal planned after National Day of Prayer is ruled unconstitutional," *The Christian Century*, 18 May 2010.

[15] Ibid.

[16] Ibid.

[17] Ibid.

Muslims in which he said, "I have expressed my concerns about the teachings of Islam regarding the treatment of women and the killing of non-Muslims or infidels."[18] At one point he had also said that Islam was "evil and wicked."[19]

The Pentagon bowed to the pressure and "disinvited" Graham as the speaker. Following that there was some movement to keep him from being involved in the National Day of Prayer.

Discussion Questions for Scenario 9

1. What is the Soul Freedom issue here for Franklin Graham?
2. Was he right to have said what he did say?
3. Do his remarks reflect bias or an awareness of truth?
4. What are the limits of ecumenicity?
5. Should there be any limits?
6. Do you think Graham should have been disinvited? Why? Why not?
7. Should the Muslims have been more open and tolerant?

---

[18] Ken Garfield, "Graham stands by comments on Islam: But 'evil and wicked' quote doesn't cancel Christian love, he says," *The Charlotte Observer*, September 19, 2001.

[19] Ibid.

8

Regenerate Church Membership

I grew up on the south shore of Massachusetts, meaning Plymouth, and the Puritans were a part of my consciousness. This was before the tourist bureau put a replica of the Mayflower in Plymouth Harbor, and before protests on Thanksgiving Day that called to mind the inhumane treatment of the native populations by the Puritans who identified the natives as "savages" and related to them accordingly. I don't even remember Plymouth Plantation and its recreation of the early township with its protecting fort on Fort Hill. I do remember standing by Plymouth Rock on cold days when the biting wind would come in from the ocean, and I would be viscerally reminded of the hardships the Puritans endured.

I also remember the Puritan church they formed. I was a Baptist growing up, but I had some friends who attended the Randolph Congregational Church in the center of town. Because our Baptist church held summer worship services with the Congregationalists, we had a number of church connections.

I did take note that my Congregational friends, like our Roman Catholic friends, had been baptized as infants, so growing up they were members of their church. This seemed strange to me because we Baptists did not join the church until after baptism, which for most of us seemed to occur as we entered our junior high years. Each year our church held a membership class for those in the seventh grade.

I came to understand in later years the idea of confirmation as that time when the individual "confirmed" his or her baptism and made it his or her own. It may have been my perception, but it did not seem that confirmation was approached with the same kind of seriousness with which we approached our baptism. After all, this was a serious decision that would affect the remainder of our lives. My friends did not seem to have the same kind of angst; confirmation appeared to be something that was more pro-forma. I know that many churches do a very fine job with confirmation, making it real and important, but suffice it to say, that is not my memory.

I could see problems inherent in this arrangement, that came into focus when, in either college or seminary, we were talking about what the early Puritans in Massachusetts called the "half-way covenant."

It seemed that full membership in the Puritan Congregational Church demanded a conversion experience—some kind of proof that there had been a personal experience of God at work in their lives through Jesus Christ, and that a commitment had been made to accept the offer of salvation so freely offered. This was no problem for the early Puritans. Strongly religious, this was part of who they were.

But, sadly, it did not prove as true for their children and grandchildren. This is my own personal experience, and it is so for many others as well. We all know of situations where children brought up in a religious family do not experience or understand faith as their parents experienced and understood it. They may end up in church or they may not end up in church, but much of the time they do not have the same intensity of personal, life-changing conversion and the evangelical furor it creates. These children simply grew up in the faith; this does not always make it less real; but many times it makes it less passionate, and sometimes it makes it simply pro-forma.

This created a problem for the Puritan Congregationalists; their children and grand-children had been baptized as children, but they did not give evidence of God's Spirit at work in their lives to certify them for full membership. The practice of what came to be called "the half-way covenant" was the answer to this problem. Family members baptized at birth could stay in the church by means of the half-way covenant, which meant they could become members in the church and their children could be baptized. The only thing that they could not do was participate in some of the business matters of the church. They were restricted from voting on certain financial matters and/or the calling of a new minister for the parish.

In the end, you find that you have a church filled with members who have come in the side door; they have the inheritance of faith, they were raised in the faith. All they lacked were strong religious convictions. In terms of one of the old analogies from the sixties, the church becomes "a club" as opposed to a life-saving mission.

Baptists saw this differently, and at our best we still do. Baptists postpone baptism until the individual reaches what we call the "age of responsibility." By this we mean the age when they are old and aware enough to make their own decision to acknowledge the work of God in their lives, the presence of God in their lives, the saving grace of Jesus Christ at work in their lives. This is regenerate church membership. This means that church membership consists of those who have had an experience of God, who have testified publicly to that experience, who give evidence of that experience at work in their lives, who request baptism by immersion as another public declaration of this faith, and who then take part in the work and ministry of the church.

Membership in the church, then, is not "inherited." It is not something that comes to us as a right. Membership follows a sequence: First, there is the preaching of the Word, then there is the acceptance of the Word by the individual, then there is the public profession of faith before the church, and finally is there baptism and membership. As Baptists we are called upon to continue to ensure the validity of this sequence in our practice, resisting the temptation to baptize people simply because church membership requires it, or a youth has reached the age of accountability and it is "time."

We come to God, to transforming faith in God, by different paths. For some of us, it is a growing-up experience; raised in the faith, we come to learn how much it means to us, how important it is to our lives, and we move right into it. For others there is a powerful, life-changing experience that can be tremendously emotional. This experience is brought on by a sense of personal sin accompanied by terrible guilt, followed by a powerful sense of God's forgiveness and love that is experienced as God's saving grace. Both are equally real. The grace is that we find our individual way to God's presence and commit our lives to live and work in the world as faithful disciples. We must understand that neither is normative, that indeed there are many gates to the City of God.

Church Discipline

In the first scenario, with the section on regenerate church membership, I will attempt, amongst other things, to have you grapple with the practice in many Baptist churches of church discipline. There is certainly not as much of this today as there was in perhaps the last couple of centuries, but it is a legitimate practice, and most books on Baptist Polity I have read mention it.

Church discipline is born of the idea of a regenerate church membership. Believers coming into the life of the church have been touched, if not transformed, by the power of God's Holy Spirit. With this they are eager to grow in their faith and to be ardent in its practice. Experience tells us, however, that maintaining this ardent fervor through spiritual discipline calls for constant action and attentiveness, and with busy schedules and living in a world of temptations there is sometimes a tendency to fall away from the original passion. Historically the church has identified this as "falling into sin" or "backsliding."

The question then focuses on the desirability of maintaining the freshness of the regenerate church experience when surrounded by others who are having personal difficulties and falling short of it. Another way of looking at it is, how does one keep the "purity" of the church?

Dealing with the individual or individuals in terms of loving correction is known as church discipline. "Church discipline may be broadly defined as the confrontive and corrective measures taken by an individual, church leaders, or the congregation regarding a matter of sin in the life of a believer."[1] This can be done quietly, one-on-one, between two people within the life of the church, or it can involve the action of a governing board with representatives sent to lovingly confront an individual or individuals about a bothersome matter, or it could be an issue brought for action to an entire congregation. It is not to be seen as punitive, but rather as an attempt to bring those confronted back into a state of regenerate church membership and fellowship within the church.

Church discipline and the call for it is found in a number of scriptural passages, but a good example can be found in Paul's first letter to the church at Corinth (1 Co 5:1–13). Chapter five begins with a situation of sexual immorality. Paul states that he has judged the individual involved and the church is to deal with the situation because "a little yeast leavens the whole batch of dough" (1 Co 5:6). He next speaks of not associating with those in the world who are sexually

---

[1] Carl Laney, *A Guide to Church Discipline* (Grand Rapids MI: Bethany House Publishers) 14.

immoral, and concludes, "But now I am writing to you not to associate with anyone who bears the name of brother or sister who is sexually immoral or greedy, or is an idolater, reviler, drunkard, or robber. Do not even eat with such a one" (1 Co 5:11). We would note here that Paul's list of sins is not singular, but interestingly inclusive; he does not rank them in a hierarchy. They are equally sinful and equally punishable.[2]

In today's language we would call church discipline "tough love." The Amish in their Baptist roots would call this "shunning."

Those who would practice church discipline claim to be driven by two different realities beyond the scriptural admonition. The first reality is internal within the life of the church. Here they might quote the old farmer who would say, "one bad apple eventually spoils the entire barrel" or they might quote Paul "a little yeast leavens the whole batch of dough" (1 Co 5:6). I have heard church discipline described as similar to a cancer operation; as painful as it may be, unless the cancer is removed there cannot be health in the body. Practitioners of church discipline might also cite the influence of a bad example, and would, of course, insist on their interest as a loving act of hopeful restoration, of seeking and returning as in the parable of Jesus with the lost sheep.

The second reality is external, trying to protect the church from having its witness and testimony destroyed by a person from within living a corrupted form of faith and making the church vulnerable to the community condemnation of hypocrisy, as in "see how they fail to live up to those principles they preach to us."

The results of discipline can range from censure to expulsion, so it is a very serious matter indeed. Its purpose is to maintain a regenerate church membership.

Church discipline is not without its problems. I have seen magazine articles of churches sued for making an issue public by expelling a member from the church. The person expelled argued that their reputation had been damaged in the community when the church made public their condemnation in what otherwise should have been a private

---

[2] Remember this as you read other sections of this book when the question is asked after some of the scenarios if Paul is an equal opportunity judge. Does he rank certain sins above others? He certainly is an equal opportunity judge here; there is not even the hint of ranking them!

and personal matter. As individuals within church life, we have seen excessive judgmentalism unrestrained by love and/or compassion. We have seen personal vendetta turned into accusations of spiritual infraction in the life of another, hoping the discipline process will be personally satisfying to the accuser. We have seen judgment tempered by culture rather than by Scriptural Authority. We have seen situations where the judgment or action violates what some would believe to be Soul Freedom or Biblical Authority principles.

Also think about this possibility: There might be times when the one thought to be in need of discipline could be a genuine prophetic voice that the church needs to hear, but does not want to hear.

Also problematical here is the stringency in many places of the personal privacy laws that prohibit the sharing of private information in the public place. Before my retirement, we put limits on even releasing the name of a person who was in the hospital, and the fact that they were in the hospital, without express permission from the individual. Many were irate when they called in to ask about a fellow church member, and were told that the information could not be shared.

When I was in seminary, I wanted to write a paper on the history of my home church in Randolph, Massachusetts, to fulfill one of my independent study courses. When I asked, the church leaders were delighted to give me access to some of the original documents. I will never forget finding the record of a vote asking certain members of the church to go and call on one of the sisters. They were to advise her that her relationship with the church was in jeopardy and that, unless she changed her ways, the church would remove the hand of fellowship from her. I was even more surprised when I found out that her "sin" had been nodding off in church. It didn't seem to me to warrant that kind of action, and I jokingly said to Fred Knox, my pastor, that she probably had fallen asleep during the sermon, or even worse, the offering. In succeeding years I have wondered to what extent church disciple might be rooted in culture, or even in petulance or arrogance.

This is certainly not to minimize the fact that we all are confronted with serious issues within church life that demand some kind of attention from us as church leaders, or from the church body itself. Walking a line governed by judgment, love, grace, and forgiveness is never easy.

Over the years I have never asked the churches I served to exercise discipline over a member, nor have any of my churches asked it of me. This is not to say that there haven't been heart-to-heart conversations with individuals over certain matters, definite expressions of concern, but we have always felt that expressions of love in the privacy of a one-on-one relationship has been the best way to deal with the situations with which we were confronted. We are cognizant, of course, of the mandate to be as loving, caring, and forgiving as Jesus would. The prayer "forgive us our sins as we forgive those who sin against us" is an awesome reminder of God's expectations of us, and I have said more than once from the pulpit that we ought to be "in fear and trembling" each Sunday morning as we repeat this phrase in the Lord's Prayer.

I might also say that while recognizing church discipline as "removing a bad apple" or "surgically removing a tumor" or "yeast leavening the dough," there is also the possibility, and it is here that we place our hopes, that there is power in agape love to transform and change once again, and we cite the joy in the parable of Jesus around the finding of a lost coin (Lk 15:8–10),[3] or the joy of a father running to meet his wayward son who has come home (Lk 15:11–32). Two of my three churches have been large enough to hold multiple morning worship services, and in the larger church I find that people and personal issues don't take on the angst of the smaller church where everything is more transparent. There is, in the larger church, much more room for anonymity, and I suspect that this may mean a lot more room for grace. (Rereading this I find this last statement to be a little bit provocative; I will leave it in, however, and throw it at you as a discussion question. What do you think about it? Is living out in grace more difficult in the smaller church than it is in the larger?)

Topics for Discussion

Regenerate Church Membership Scenario 1

After the latest meeting of the board of deacons, a delegation is instructed to bring a matter to the attention of the pastor and the church

[3] Verse 10 states: "Just so, I tell you, there is joy in the presence of the angels of God over one sinner who repents."

board. There are several members of the board who are quite concerned with the spiritual state of a number of the church members, a state evidenced by their lack of attendance and participation. There are also more specific rumors about some who have "fallen into sin." Is it your imagination that several deacons seem to get a perverse pleasure from detailing these allegations at some length? Quoting Scripture where Paul says that the Church should break fellowship with those who might be stumbling blocks to others in the congregation, they ask for the church to consider returning to the practice of church discipline, that is meeting with these individuals and laying things on the line, calling for repentance and participation or being disfellowshiped from the body. They remind you that historically many Baptist churches have practiced this form of church discipline.

Discussion Questions for Scenario 1

1. What do you think is going on with the board of deacons? Do you think they are being Scriptural?
2. Do you think that they are being over-zealous?
3. Do you think that they are becoming more personally intrusive than they have a right to be?
4. What do you personally believe about the act of church discipline? Would you be for it? Why? Would you be against it? Why?
5. Would it be appropriate to remind them of what other portions of Scripture say, where for example, Jesus speaks of love and forgiveness seventy times seven, without limit?
6. Do you remind the deacons that we are not to judge, and if we do God will judge us with that same judgment: "Forgive us our sins as we forgive those who sin against us."
7. Do you remind the deacons that we are all sinners before God, that sin is sin, and that no sin is greater than any other sin?
8. If you agree to meet with people whose attendance and/or behavior is in question, what kind of approach do you take with them? Do you tell them that you have missed them? Do you bring to their attendance your awareness of their sinful state? Do you warn them that they need to find forgiveness and

reconciliation? Do you ask them to stop attending church until this is resolved?

9. Do you tell them that you will remove them from the membership role of the church as a statement of the church's conviction?
10. Do you offer to put them on the prayer list?
11. What do you say if they offer to put you and the church on their prayer list?
12. Do you think that confrontation is a good way to get someone to change? What might be the price that you pay for confrontation?
13. What is the danger of ignoring a problem?
14. What do you think a person meant, who had just been involved in a confrontation with a church member over an issue, "We wept the entire time!"
15. Do you think that in some instances we are like the Puritan Congregationalists, allowing children of family members to join our churches by "inheritance" rather than by a strong personal experience of faith?

Regenerate Church Membership Scenario 2

Your church has several young people who want to be baptized, but those who make the baptism decision on behalf of the church feel that in spite of their expression, they are not ready to take that step. The church cites many reasons that the young people want to be baptized: peer pressure, parental pressure, and the strong influence of a member of the church staff. However, they see a lack of evidence in their individual lives, and much immaturity.

Discussion Questions for Scenario 2

1. As a church, how do we nurture young people in the faith? How do we acknowledge with young people the different stages of faith? How do we encourage them that it is all right to be where they are? How do we define and move them along to next steps?
2. In regenerate church membership what constitutes regeneration? Are there signs? If there are what might they be? How do we allow for personal differences?

3. Does answering "yes" to the question: Do you accept Jesus Christ as your Savior and Lord—mean the same thing as a powerful and profound Holy Spirit generated experience of God?
4. Do all of our faith experiences have to be the same?
5. How does the church allow for latitude in the variety of faith experiences that are presented to us?
6. What does it mean to be a "one size fits all" church?

Regenerate Church Membership Scenario 3

In my concluding remarks for this chapter I said: "In the larger church I find that people and personal issues don't take on the angst of the smaller church where everything is more transparent. There is in the larger church much more room for anonymity and I suspect that this may mean a lot more room for grace."

Discussion Questions for Scenario 3

1. Do you agree that there are differences in the personality of the large, versus the smaller church?
2. Why is it that the smaller church cannot encourage anonymity?
3. What are the elements of the larger church that make anonymity pervasive?

Commentary on Scenario 3

I believe in the principle of church discipline. It is a logical action given what we believe about regenerate church membership. If we understand the nature of temptation, then the means of maintaining the wholesomeness of the regenerate church is logical. Its practice in the New Testament Church also is important, as Paul wrote to suggest the removal of those who were a threat to the sanctity of the church body. I believe, also, in tough love; there are times when a family or a corporate body has to draw a behavioral line, believing that the acting is positive and saving, as opposed to negative and destructive. I believe that the church discipline process, if and when practiced, has to be founded in sacred conviction, in thoughtful prayer, in discerning what is right and best for the Church and hopefully for the individual to be disciplined.

At the same time, I never remember a time when I practiced church discipline in any of the four churches in which I served in forty years of ministry. Nor was I aware of it being a part of any of the Baptist churches with which I was familiar.

The reasons for the difference between belief and practice are found in several areas.

First, I am troubled by judgmentalism. I have found that the human family is very quick to judge, that judgment is not always neutral, that judgment can be impelled by personal animus and vengeance. I am bothered by the times that I have made a judgment and that has proven to be a serious error on my part as time has passed. I am aware that pronounced judgments are very difficult to retract or to have evidence of them erased, and damage can be significant. I am sensitive to the admonition of Jesus that we judge only as we want others to judge us; I find the line in the Lord's Prayer, "forgive us our sins as we forgive those who sin against us" to be terrifying when I really think about it. I have seen too many times when our human frailties get in the way of that perfect discerning process.

Second, I find the love and grace of Jesus in the New Testament to be pervasive. He defended and did not judge the woman caught in adultery (Jn 7:53–8:11). Jesus was judged by the scribes and Pharisees because he welcomed all sinners (Lk 15:1–2), refusing to condemn them. He seemed publicly to err on the side of love, and I think that if that was good enough for Jesus, then it might not be a bad practice for me.

Third, I have stuck in my mind an argument from college days. We were debating in Christian legalistic terms the drinking of alcoholic beverages. The pervasive argument was that if personal consumption of alcohol was a stumbling block to any, then refraining from use was mandatory, so great was the obligation to the weaker Christian. Then someone found that reformed theologian John Murray[4] had come to this argument from a different perspective. He stated that the use of alcohol was banned neither by Jesus nor Paul; only the excessive use was faulted, as was the excessive use of food, amongst other things. Murray's point was that the weaker faith of a sister or brother that kept an individual

[4] Born in Scotland, Murray taught at Princeton Theological Seminary and left to become one of the founders of the Westminster Theological Seminary.

from alcohol use was, in fact, a stumbling block to their stronger faith. I know the argument is a bit sophistic, but it became an important reminder to me to see two sides of a question, and that rushes to judgment and action were more often born in issues of culture, or dogmatism.

Realistically I found that many of the issues where discipline might have been appropriate resolved themselves with one or more of the following solutions:

—With individual and wider family conversations,
—With provision of counseling services to help with life issues,
—With the simple passage of time,
—Or with the individual removing themselves, and becoming increasingly uncomfortable within the setting of the Church.

Regenerate Church Membership Scenario 4

One morning when you pick up your newspaper you notice a front-page article about registered sex offenders. As you read it, you are shocked to discover the name of one of the more prominent members of your church. Though you had been a member of that church for a number of years, you had no more than the most casual relationship with the individual. Still, the paper's declaration was news to you, and as you asked around, his situation was not known within the church.

Subsequent newspaper articles explore his areas of involvement within the church and community, and questions are asked about his insulation from particular areas that might produce temptation. At the same time, some of the members of the church are concerned about it being a safe place for children and teens, and there are some feelings expressed that it might be a good idea if this man would move on.

Then there is an article in which the church's pastor is prominently quoted as saying that no action will be taken by the church. The church understands that the man has a past and that his past is troublesome. At the same time the church believes in the power of the gospel to transform an individual into a new creation. If there were a "smoking gun" of inappropriate behavior, the church would certainly look into the matter. But absent such an incriminating piece of evidence, the church will firmly support his individual right to be there.

Discussion Questions for Scenario 4

1. What are you thinking as you read this?
2. Is your gut telling you something different than your mind?
3. Do you believe in the power of the Gospel to transform an individual? Do you ever get suspicious of that process? Do you ever get the feeling that some people abuse it?
4. Would you feel that the church should take no precautions? Some precautions? Complete precautions?
5. Is the pastor courageous? Or foolish?
6. Ronald Reagan once said, "Trust, but verify!" How would you apply that admonition here?

9

The Separation of Church and State

Some years ago a young man came to the United States from a country in the Middle East. He came to enjoy the fruits of education, and he enrolled at a major university. While he was here, he took the opportunity to taste the American way of life. This individual was an Arab by ethnicity; he was a Muslim by religious faith.

In the beginning he was curious, for everything seemed so different. By the end of the first semester he was disturbed. By the end of the year he was troubled. At the beginning of the second year he was agitated. By the time he returned home he was angry.

The reasons for his behavior, for his emotional response, for the conclusions he began to formulate, emerged out of what he saw at work in American life, especially as it pertained to the freedom of choice that was inherent in the culture and life style for every person. Americans could dress according to their preference; they could, for example, wear bathing suits at the beach that he, quite frankly, thought were obscene. Americans could worship, or not worship, in the place of their choice. Americans could believe or not believe in God; they could range from being an atheist to being a fundamentalist, and anywhere in the spectrum was all right. Americans could read the Bible or not read the Bible; they could interpret the Bible in a variety of ways; there was no one authority that said it had to be read a certain way or that there was a specific doctrine or dogma or teaching to be followed.

He found no agreement with these beliefs. It was his conviction that there was a standard, that there was a single way that had to be interpreted, and that indeed, the way had to be enforced if necessary.

He believed that God, whom he named Allah, was lord over the entire universe. He believed that Allah was due absolute obedience, and that Allah had put down the principles of this obedience in his book, the Koran. On its pages it clearly taught how individuals, families, and societies should live, how there should be no disagreement about these standards, and how there should be complete obedience to them. The arbitrators were the clergy, and the government should consist entirely of clergy at the highest levels so that the civil authority could implement, by force if necessary, the way of life and faith that should be lived on a daily basis. There was no option not to believe. There was no option not to practice.

He was appalled by what we call the Separation of Church and State—of calling for two separate entities independent in their individual organization, action, and responsibility. When he got back home, he began to write about his feelings, his observations, and what he wrote became the guidebook for many radical Muslims like himself. The goal of their radical religious faith is to establish societies, theocracies, around the world. These are to be ruled by the law of God as interpreted by the clergy and the Koran. It is their belief, their absolute conviction, that societies that are disobedient to this should be forced into obedience or judged and, therefore, destroyed.

The above illustration is not meant to vilify Islam. In 2000, Karen Armstrong published a book suggesting that all forms of fundamentalism, whether Islamic, Jewish, or Christian, held common radical ideals from their different religious biases.[1] There are numerous religious groups that chafe at what we know as First Amendment principles concerning public prayer, public display of religious symbols, and legislation on issues such as abortion, to name a few.

The theocratic ideal where religion and government are bound together is strongly and passionately held, to the point that creating or enforcing it has brought enormous violence into our world in these years. It is, however, an ideal that we Baptists turned away from at the time of the Reformation. The Separation of Church and State that we hold so dear is interesting stuff indeed.

At the time of the Reformation, the Church and the state (government) were inseparable. In this relationship, the Church held enormous power that was both political/secular and spiritual. The Church used the state to enforce its religious beliefs and its moral values. It used the state to enforce a singular religion, and dissent was a political matter as much as a religious one. It was the governmental authorities that burned heretics at the stake for dissonant views. On the other hand,

---

[1] Karen Armstrong, *The Battle For God* (New York: Random House, 2000).

the state used the Church to give it a moral, religious credibility—an imprimatur of respectability. The leadership of the state had the recognition and support of religious leaders, and in many instances, it was the religious leaders who inaugurated them into their posts or offices.

Reading the Scriptures, believers during the time of the Reformation began to see another model of belief and action, one that was contrary to what was then being practiced. There were two emergent principles that were to call into question the Church/state relationship.

The first principle is that of the Priesthood of the Individual Believer; this says that we have direct access to God through the life and work of Jesus Christ, so that we do not need any other external intermediators such as Church and clergy. The second principle is the idea of Soul Freedom; this says that no external authority can tell us what the elements of faith and belief should be; we have the competency to discover biblical truth and faith behavior for ourselves, and, indeed, that is a God-given responsibility that we bear. Church and state separation, is emergent from, or an end result of, these first two principles.

The first byproduct of two separate bodies, Church and state, is a free Church. In this, Church believers must be free to stand before God in their own merit. Additionally they must be free to interpret the Scripture by their own process of study, conversation, and prayer, and to live their lives by the dictates of their conscience before God. With all of this they must bind together as the Church with total freedom to act out these convictions. Walter Shurden has defined it thus: "Church freedom is the historic Baptist affirmation that local churches are free, under the Lordship of Christ, to determine their membership and leadership, to order their worship and work, to ordain whom they perceive as gifted for ministry, male or female, and to participate in the larger Body of Christ, of whose unity and mission Baptists are proudly a part."[2]

A second byproduct is a state or government that is not required to carry out the principles, or enforce the practices, of the Church. It is not the role of state to legislate or enforce morality, polity, or practice. The

---

[2] Walter G. Shurden, *The Baptist Identity: Four Fragile Freedoms* (Macon GA: Smyth & Helwys Publishing, 1993) 33.

state has clearly defined functions to carry out, and its responsibilities are limited to these specific functions.

To put it succinctly, the state must not be the tool of the Church, and the Church must not be the tool of the state.

The people who began to believe this way became known as "Separatists" because they separated themselves from the established Church and if they could, from the government that existed in that time and place. This was the impetus for the settlement of the New World. The settlers sailed across oceans and suffered immeasurable hardships so that they could establish their societies as they saw fit. These societies were the public body that would incorporate into their functions the private intuitive and spiritual process. The public or corporate life modeled that which was private and personal. The key was separateness and individuality that then expanded into the independence of the body of Christ.

It is profoundly ironic that while the Pilgrims enjoyed this religious freedom, they did not allow others of differing views to participate in it, as Roger Williams discovered when he was banned from Massachusetts Colony—forced, due to his dissident views, to flee into the wilderness in the midst of a stern winter, believing that the unyielding forest would be kinder to him that the unyielding Puritans.[3]

Through the influence of prominent Virginia Baptist John Leland, along with other Baptists, the Baptist ideas of Church and state separation were written into the First Amendment of the Constitution: "Congress shall make no law respecting the establishment of religion." In Baptist dialogue on this subject, you will hear again and again references to the Establishment Clause, and this is what is meant by it.

One of the key leaders in the Separation of Church and State issue was Isaac Backus; Backus had founded a Baptist congregation in

---

[3] A recent book has chronicled this rigid fundamentalism of the Puritan church which demanded conformity of the residents of the Massachusetts Commonwealth, to the degree that dissenters were harshly beaten and even in some instances put to death. A death sentence was issued against Roger Williams for his divergent views and his unwillingness to recant them. That book is: John M. Barry, *Roger Williams and The Creation of the American Soul: Church, State, and the Birth of Liberty* (New York, Viking, 2012.)

Middleboro, Massachusetts, in 1756. There, he was to take umbrage with the policy of the Commonwealth of Massachusetts, which taxed its citizens in support of the "official" state church, the Congregational Church of the Puritans. He was to argue his cause of separation with both the Massachusetts Court and later the Continental Congress, declaring that he and his fellow Baptists should not be penalized for refusing to support what he considered to be a false religion. He wrote vociferously on the matter, and though complete religious liberty in Massachusetts did not come until after his death, he was able to have laws passed that allowed Baptists to sue the Commonwealth so their tax dollars could go to the Baptist church instead of the Congregational.[4]

Speaking of the Separation of Church and State, Isaac Backus said in 1773: "Church and state are separate, the effects are happy, and they do not at all interfere with each other; but where they have been confounded together, no tongue nor pen can fully describe the mischiefs (sic) that have ensued."[5] In our own time, Baptist Brent Walker said: "I must not insist that government promote my religion if I don't want the government to promote somebody else's religion, and I should not permit government to harm someone else's religion if I don't want government to harm my religion."[6]

Despite the Establishment Clause and our belief in the Separation of Church and State, there is, however, a role for the government just as there is a role for the Church. The government has the power to defend the nation by every means possible, and the government has the authority to establish just laws for order in society. All of this authority is derived from God, and we would cite two sources, realizing that there is more on this question in the Soul Freedom chapter. The first citation comes from Romans 13:1, "Let every person be subject to the governing

---

[4] For some of this information on Isaac Backus I am indebted to The Reformed Leader, found at www.reformedleader.org/backus.htm.

[5] This quote by Isaac Backus was found in an article on Baptists in Wikipedia.
http://en.wikipedia.org/wiki/Separation_of_church_and_state_in_the_United_States

[6] Brent Walker is the Executive Director of the Baptist Joint Committee for Religious Liberty, located in Washington, DC. I found this quote in an article he had written for one of the issues of *Report from the Capital.*

authorities; for there is no authority except from God, and those authorities that exist have been instituted by God." Our second citation is from 1 Peter 2:1–2, "For the Lord's sake accept the authority of every human institution, whether of the emperor as supreme, or of governors, as sent by him to punish those who do wrong and to praise those who do right."

Yet, clearly, the authority given by God to civil government has its limitations—it can never be exercised at the expense of faith. Obedience to the civil authority is always subservient to the authority of conscience and of belief, as determined by the individual in their walk with the Holy Spirit. Never can civil authority come in conflict with the relationship of the individual with their Lord. When that choice is forced, faith has to be preemptive. Here we would cite Acts 4:19 and Acts 5:29. In both instances, the civil authorities have put a limitation on the actions of, first, Peter and John, and then Peter and the disciples—and the disciples have disobeyed the order. When asked why, they boldly testify that, "We must obey God rather than any human authority." In matters of conscience faith in action will trump law and government every time.

On the other hand, the Church is to be the place where the soul encounters God, where worship takes place, where faith is explored and challenged, where our ideas of faith and practice are tested against the ideas of others and a consensus of belief and practice is sustained. The Church is where growth in the journey of faith takes place.

Civil Disobedience

When an individual stands up and declares to the state "the law you have created, or the action you have initiated, or the practice which you are establishing, is a violation of my conscience and interpretation of the Scripture, and I must disobey this law because of who I am and because of who God calls me to be," this is what we know as civil disobedience. Civil disobedience is willful failure to obey a law because the conscience denies the law's right to existence, or it is a willful breaking of a law in protest as a way of calling the attention of the civil authority to what you feel is a mistake in public policy and action.

This leads us directly to another issue that I want to touch upon. The issue asks the question as to whether or not those who exercise their Soul Freedom with an expression that pushes on the principle of

Separation of Church and State, should be able to act in civil disobedience, that is break the law, without punishment.[7] I remember during the Vietnam War how a number of people known to me picked the tax on telephone service as being symbolic of governmental authority and refused to pay it because the taxes were being used to support what was considered by them to be an unjust war. I remember Gordon Torgerson, who, at that time, was the senior minister of First Baptist Church of Worcester, Massachusetts, explaining this and his reasons to a group of us. It is not my intention to answer why they picked the telephone tax—there may have been a specific reason but I do not remember it. My point is, that the federal government did not take kindly to their action, and they paid the tax eventually through being taken to court, or having judgments filed against them, or by confiscation of their assets. There was no civil disobedience without consequences.

Likewise, the Berrigan Brothers were on the FBI's most-wanted list. Eventually they were apprehended and sent to jail for their civil disobedience in regards to what they did to draft records: They broke into federal offices where draft records were secured and poured blood on the records. Those, who because of conscience, burned their draft cards and sought to elude the draft eventually ended up in Canada to avoid the penalties that were being thrown at them. Eventually, under the presidency of Jimmy Carter, they were offered amnesty, and many were able to return to the United States without penalty.

In a scenario in the Soul Freedom chapter there is the story of how, back in the middle of the nineteenth century, Henry David Thoreau ended up in jail for his failure to pay the Poll Tax. By and large, protest by reason of conscience exacts a penalty; Soul Freedom and Separation of Church and State do not grant immunity from prosecution. Take the stand and you must be willing to take the consequences.

Practical Applications of the Separation of Church and State

---

[7] We note that there is a scenario in the chapter on Soul Freedom, and several scenarios in this chapter that deal concretely with the issue of civil disobedience and punishment.

There are several places where the tension of Church and state is being played out today. I will take five issues and give you a spectrum of interpretation.

The first issue is public school prayer. On one side, people say that of course we must allow our children to pray publicly in school; teaching them about God is a part of the education process. Children and schools have been doing this since the founding of our nation. No, the purists say, that kind of prayer should be taking place in the home and church. When you read from a Scripture in the classroom as we used to do when I was in grade school, when you pray to the Christian God as we used to do in grade school, then you are establishing a religion, and you are denying to others who are not of like mind their Soul Freedom and Priesthood. You could argue, I suppose that we were all the same back in those childhood years, and in that small Randolph community of 1945 and following we *were* all the same. We were all white, and we were all Christian, but of course, for the principle, that is not the point.

The second issue is the pledge of allegiance to the flag of the United States. A California federal court ruled not long ago that "under God" was in violation of the principle of the establishment clause in the Constitution (First Amendment). There was an outcry. The Christians said, "Of course we must affirm our nation is under God." Here again I have heard people refer back to the founding fathers of our nation. With this Ben Franklin is often quoted as having said during the Constitutional Convention, "Unless the Lord build the house, they labor in vain that build it" (Ps 127:1 KJV). This is then used to prove that the religious faith of the founding fathers is built into our country's warp and woof, something certainly for us to emulate.

Those not Christian would counter this with: "You are making me say something, affirm something, which I do not believe to be true. You are interfering with my freedom of faith (or lack of faith). They would claim a religion is being established and that they were being coerced into a particular circle of faith to which they did not desire inclusion.

The third issue is abortion. There are some who say this is a moral evil and we must legislate against it towards protection of the unborn fetus. We note that we must give them the right to this conclusion and their desire to defend it, for it is indeed a matter that emerges out of their study of Scripture, and it is an exercise of their freedom of conscience.

At the same time, on the other side there are those who say that freedom of choice is a gift from the Creator to the creation. This is their conclusion from their study of Scripture and it is their very strong belief that their personal freedom of conscience to inform and act upon such a choice outweighs every other consideration. A law against abortion, they believe would enforce a religious bias, and that bias would trump soul freedom; again it would violate the establishment clause because it would be enforcing religious and moral values.

We would note the tension between these two polar opposite opinions, each drawing conclusions from Scripture (both quote from the Bible, although different parts, to buttress their views). This is an excellent example of the tension between Soul Freedom and Biblical Authority. Those who would put Soul Freedom preeminent would be agreeable to the tension; those with strong convictions on Biblical Authority would believe it a moral cause to buttress their biblical views with civil law, believing also that in pursuing the law, they would be doing God's work.

The fourth issue is homosexuality and the legalization of gay marriage. There are some who say that the Bible speaks against the practice of homosexuality, and, therefore, we should pass legislation prohibiting what God does not allow. There are others who say that God made some people this way, gay or lesbian, and they should have a right to practice as they are created. Gays and lesbians should not be refused the intimacy and civil benefits that come with marriage. Again, as in issue number four, there is a tension here between Soul Freedom Christians and Biblical Authority Christians.

The fifth issue is the support of private schools, or more generally religious schools. Decades ago religious education was limited to parochial schools, but many independent churches now have extensive education complexes. There is one side that says, "If we want to educate our children this way we have the freedom to do this—and you should pay the school what you are saving in the public school. To do this would really make no difference to the taxpayer." The other side says, "No, this is sectarian education that is influenced by the Church. It teaches Church principle and dogma. As such it is the establishment of religion, so it cannot be sustained by public funds."

There was an interesting twist on this not too long ago in our morning newspaper, the *Indianapolis Star*. The Roman Catholic diocese of Indiana is facing financial shortfalls, and to save money is interested in closing several of its parochial schools. This has met some opposition from the families who have children in the schools where closing is being discussed. The newspaper article spoke of one particular school that was talking to the city about the possibility of becoming a charter school, and thus eligible for city financing. The ruling was that this could be done if the religious symbols—cross, crucifix, and the like—were removed from the entire building. The new charter school could use the same building and the identical rooms, and they could maintain the same teaching staff. Though the article did not mention it, I would assume the charter school would have a governing board free from church influence, though using the same building and staff seems to cry conflict of interest. At the very least one has to admire the ingenuity of the approach.

I want to bring us back to the discussion on the five issues, and you will note that wisely I have not come down on one side or the other on these Church-state issues as I have spoken of them. I am content to show the spread, and illustrate the difficulty of Church and state separation. I remember when I used these issues to illustrate a sermon on Church and state separation, and how a number of the members of my congregation were irate that I did not tell them how to work through and solve these problems, or in other words, give them the "right" answers.[8] I will say now what I said then: "We can live with the tensions; in fact, it is important to live with these tensions. Indeed, this is what freedom is all about. You need to go to the Scripture and do your due diligence, and come to conclusions based upon your own study process." I recognize, however, that my unwillingness to provide them with concrete answers goes against today's trend of congregants looking for churches where preachers will tell them what to think and believe. Convincing

---

[8] As I remember, most of those who asked were of a more fundamentalist view, and I have to confess that I almost said to them: "To tell you the truth, you most certainly *do not want to hear* what I think and believe on these matters!" Of course a preacher with a more fundamentalist viewpoint would flip this observation 180 degrees. My point is that this ability to come from a different view and to a different conclusion is a verification of our Baptist Way. I sincerely believe that.

individuals that forcing them to think the issues through for themselves and come to their own conclusions is the Baptist way goes against the current. But such a declaration is, in fact, at the heart and soul of who we are. And with that I should be hearing the echoes of your "Amen!"

The Prophetic Role

An important consideration in our discussion of the Separation of Church and State is the prophetic nature of the Church, the need for the Church to sometimes confront the State with its wrong and say as the prophets of old did, "Thus says the Lord." We recall the story of David and Bathsheba; how David had Uriah, the husband of Bathsheba, killed in battle so his adultery with Uriah's wife would be covered up. Nathan the prophet tells the story of a greedy merchant who takes for slaughter the beloved pet lamb of a poor farmer rather than take one from his own herds. David is irate; "The man who has done this deserves to die; he shall restore the lamb fourfold, because he did this thing, and because he had no pity" (2 Sm 12:6). Then with deliberation and we suspect with incredible boldness, Nathan declares to David "You are the man!" (2 Sm 12:7) and condemns David for it. We have the tradition of Samuel and Saul, Elijah and Ahab, and a long line of prophets to follow, unafraid to speak to government with a strong dissident view, and to say this with the powerful "Thus says the Lord!"

There comes a time when an individual and/or the Church must become a conscience to the world and call upon it for the exercise of justice, integrity, and compassion. This could not happen if the individual or Church were controlled by the state; such control would force it to abrogate its responsibility and conscience.

On the other side of the coin we believe that it is wrong for the Church to demand of the government the passage of laws that would promote a particular moral view, taking away from individuals their own right and freedom to make moral choices. Areas that might fall into this category would include: abortion, gay marriage, public prayer, public display of religious symbols, and loyalty oaths. The principle, as I see it, is that we should have in all of these areas the right to decide for ourselves. You, or the government, cannot dictate or legislate against my conscience or counter to my scriptural interpretative conclusions. If the government passes a law that is in violation of my conscience, then I am called to stand with God over and against the law, because you, in fact, have established a religion. At the same time, my conscience certainly cannot dictate to your conscience and again, this is the tension in which we live as we live out our faith in many different ways.

We note that, unfortunately, our Soul Freedom interpretations of Scripture and God's intentions do not always end up on the same page, which of course, is one of the problems with freedom. Where I see that prophecy is needed, someone else may see that legislation is needed, and that is a Baptist difficulty. We would argue, however, that it is a delicious difficulty that challenges us to work, pray, and study together in love and harmony. In this we seek to find together the will of God for our lives, for our churches, and for the nations of the world, that we might dwell together in peace.

I realize that in some way this reiterates what has been said in earlier portions of this chapter. Nevertheless, it is important enough to repeat, and in fact, I would go so far as to ask you to reread the section where I ask the question about civil disobedience and immunity from prosecution. I hope I am not wrong that the readers of these chapters will find this a particularly fruitful area for lively discussion.

Topics for Discussion

Separation of Church and State Scenario 1

Shortly after what has come to be known as 9/11, a motion is made during the "other business" section of your administrative council agenda "to prominently display an American flag in our sanctuary in support of our country."

Or this: You have just returned from a conference on Baptist Principles and as you have thought about the Separation of Church and State, you have come to the conclusion that the American flag must, for Church-state reasons, be removed from the sanctuary.

Discussion Questions for Scenario 1

1. Does the sanctuary in which you worship have an American flag prominently displayed in it? What are the issues here on both sides—having a flag or not having a flag?

2. What is the principle of Separation of Church and State here and how does it relate to the situation?
3. If you had a flag in your sanctuary, and it was suggested that it be removed, what are the political pitfalls of this action within the life of the church?
4. If it were your decision to make, and you wanted to remove the flag, would it be best to go through the administrative body of your church (thus calling attention to your action) or simply removing it some day when no one is around (thinking that no one will notice that it is gone)?
5. If you advocated removing the flag, how would you explain this action to one of the World War II veterans in your church? Do you think they would understand the statement: "This freedom is what you fought for!" What do you think is meant by this statement?
6. What do you say to the person who asks with curiosity, or perhaps with abject disgust: "How can you be against the American flag? What kind of a person are you?"
7. What is meant by civil religion, the identification of the flag and democracy with the church and religious faith and action?
8. How would you vote? Flag in the sanctuary, or no flag in the sanctuary? Why?

Separation of Church and State Scenario 2

A church has a very strong segment within it that is vehemently opposed to a war that their government has entered into with another sovereign nation. They do not feel that the war meets the standard of what the Church has traditionally identified as a "just war." They feel strongly about the war itself, about the budget dollars being siphoned from domestic programs to pay for it, and most especially about the human capital, which, in their opinion, is being "wasted." In discussing what they might do, they look at the following options:

—Writing very strong critical letters to their governmental representatives both at the state and national level;

—Taking out full-page advertisements that state their opposition in the major newspapers in their region;

—Withholding a portion of their tax dollars to protest how the government is spending money on the war;

—Engaging in disruptive acts of civil disobedience that call attention to, and make strong statements about, their opposition to what they see as governmental injustice.

Discussion Questions for Scenario 2

1. What is your initial thinking as you read this scenario?
2. Which of the Baptist Principles are relevant here?
3. Which of the Baptist Principles are being affirmed by each of the proposed actions?
4. Which of the Baptist Principles are being rejected by their thinking or by the acts of the proposed actions?
5. Is there a point in these proposed actions where thinking and action cross a line into civil disobedience?
6. How does the traditional Biblical interpretation that calls us to follow in the prophetic tradition of the Old Testament intersect with Baptist Principles?
7. Where does civil disobedience intersect with Baptist Principles?
8. When would the line be crossed in supporting an issue making the action a violation of the principle of Separation of Church and State?
9. Suppose that the issue here was not that of war or "just war," but suppose that it was gay marriage, or abortion, or divorce, or the role of women in the church. How would changing the issue change the landscape and the actions proscribed?
10. Are some issues more potent than others? If yes, why? If no, why?

Separation of Church and State Scenario 3

A local church, after considerable study and dialogue, makes a decision that one candidate in particular best represents in the public positions she espouses the social and political matters that the church itself has affirmed. After full discussion, the administrative body of the church votes officially to stand behind her as a candidate. Being proactive, they do the following:

—They invite her to attend their Sunday morning worship service;

—The candidate is introduced from the pulpit by the pastor;

—The candidate is given the opportunity to speak from the pulpit to the congregation;

—The pastor, in a public announcement, proclaims her/his own personal support, and the support of the church body;

—The pastor urges those in the congregation to vote for this candidate on election day, believing that she will best bring their theological hopes and political desires before government bodies and the public at large;

—Over the signature of the pastor and the members of the governing council, a letter goes out to the congregation stating their support for the particular candidate, and giving the reasons for their recommendation. Accompanying the letter is some political publicity material provided to the church by the candidate's organization.

Discussion Questions for Scenario 3

1. Some of these suggested actions clearly cross the Separation of Church and State divide. Which of them, in your opinion, cross that line, and why?
2. How does the Baptist Principle of Separation of Church and State inform each of these situations?
3. Is there a difference between standing up for a particular issue as opposed to supporting a particular candidate?
4. What does the Internal Revenue Service have to say about such actions supportive of an individual candidate?
5. Is it wrong to invite a candidate to speak from your pulpit on a Sunday morning? What would make it wrong? And what would make it right? How does this intersect with Soul Freedom?
6. What is the difference between good citizenship where it helps church members make good decisions as a people of faith in electing governmental officials, and where it crosses the line into interference and undue influence or the establishment of religion?

7. What sanctions have been placed on churches that, in the estimation of the IRS, cross that "line of separation?"
8. In other words, what does it mean for a church to lose its tax-exempt status?

Commentary on Scenario 3

I remember the year 1960. Connie and I were going together, and we often used to drive in from Gordon College to Park Street Church in Boston on Sunday evenings to hear one of the great evangelical preachers of that time, Harold John Okenga. We were there the fall night prior to the presidential election when he preached the sermon that became famous. This sermon advocated that we could not, as people of faith, support a president who was Roman Catholic. If we did, we would be giving the power of the presidency to the Pope in Rome, a violation of everything our nation has stood for. John Kennedy, in his speech to the ministers of West Virginia, was successful in articulating the other side of that issue, of his own independence and commitment to separation.

I was called to First Baptist Church of Beverly as associate minister in the fall of 1964—the election year that Barry Goldwater and Lyndon Johnson faced off. I had only been there a couple of months when senior minister John Wilbur preached a sermon that he titled "November's Terrible Choice." In it he articulated the choice as a terrible one, but clearly thought that Lyndon Johnson was a better candidate. Over coffee the following week I told John that I thought that the sermon was pretty courageous, but I wondered why he thought he should preach it. By then we knew that there were a number in the congregation who were articulating their belief that the "terrible choice" was John's choice to preach such a sermon. That morning, John spoke of the New England Puritan tradition called the "Election Day Sermon." In that sermon it was a pastoral responsibility to look at government and society, to note what issues were that were particularly of interest to the Church, to determine where a prophetic note needed to be sounded, and, out of all of that, to boldly speak as to which of the candidates in his mind was best suited to meet the needs for the "City of God."

Separation of Church and State Scenario 4

At a meeting of the governing board of the church, one of the members with a penchant for patriotism suggests that you add a liturgical piece to the order of service that includes the pledge of allegiance to both the American and Christian flags. When asked why, he is incredulous that the answer is not self-evident. He speaks of the responsibility of Christian citizenship, of the need for religious people to connect their faith to their public persona as citizens, of the need to bless and confront with moral and religious values the stresses and problems of national life together. When you speak of the Separation of Church and State, he growls that this is what is wrong with our country and goes on to lecture you as to how Christian beliefs and values were the cornerstone upon which this nation was built.[9]

Discussion Questions for Scenario 4

1. What are your initial thoughts as you read this?
2. Were religious principles in fact the foundation of our early government? If you answer yes, articulate what you see those principles to be. If you believe there to be principles, how do they line up with the Baptist Principles we have set forth in this book?
3. What was the prevailing religious faith of the founding fathers, to the extent that we know it? Were they Christians? Deists? No religion at all? What do you think Thomas Jefferson was saying when he cut all of the miracle stories of Jesus out of the pages of his New Testament?
4. In the man's speech in the scenario, can you pick out what he says that is in violation of the principle of the Separation of Church and State?
5. When he finishes telling you his thoughts, what do you say to him?
6. If his suggestion were to be passed by the appropriate governing board of the church, would you agree to lead such pledges during the morning worship?

---

[9] You may want to revisit Separation of Church and State Scenario 1, to refresh yourself on the issues of even having a flag present in the sanctuary.

7. If you said "no" to leading such pledges, how would you answer their accusations that you are "anti-American?" Why would some conclude by your actions that you were anti-American? What would you mean when you told them that in fact, your belief is "more American" than their proposal? Do you think that any one would understand you?
8. What would you think if someone suggested that, following the pledge, the congregation should sing "Onward Christian Soldiers"? What do you think I am trying to say by asking this question?
9. What do we mean when we refer to civil religion?
10. How might that concept of civil religion apply here?

Separation of Church and State Scenario 5

You are in a major department store stocking up on gift items at the significant pre-Christmas sale prices. With arms full, you approach the checkout line and find yourself with two other customers in front of you.

After the sales clerk bags the items for the first person in line, she hands over the bag and declares in a robust voice, "Happy Holidays."

The second person in line half turns to you and says, "that is what is wrong with this country. We are losing the deep meaning of our faith. That's taking Christ out of Christmas, stripping this holiday of its deepest meaning and significance. We should be declaring 'Merry Christmas', not 'Happy Holidays'." The rant continues as the individual moves on to speaking about values and ideals and religion and faith and obeying God and witnessing to others.

Discussion Questions for Scenario 5

1. Your reaction is one or more of the following: You quietly say, "Amen." You emphatically say, "Praise the Lord!" You think that you can hardly wait to get home to tell your spouse about the religious nut you encountered at the store. You think to yourself, "This is too far out. I'm not going to get involved." You look at the clerk and say, "You are obviously a Baptist." You look at the person in front of you and say, "You are obviously not a Baptist." You counter their rant with a quiet discourse on the meaning of Christians living in a pluralistic society, with

emphasis on toleration and respect of those who have formed religious ideas foreign to your own, teaching them basic constitutional law—and Baptist Principle—about Congress (the state) not establishing a specific religion.

2. Run down each of the above responses and articulate how that response fits in with the principle of Church and State Separation?

Separation of Church and State Scenario 6

A number of years ago, there was a Baptist church on the south side of Indianapolis (Indianapolis Baptist Temple) that declared itself to be independent and fundamentalist. Its pastor was Greg Dixon, and for years he was an icon in the independent church movement. The church's success in reaching out to the community through bus ministry was unparalleled at that time, and the church got a lot of wonderful press as to how it was building itself into one of the largest churches in the area. At its height it had more than eight thousand members.

The church came under the conviction (Soul Freedom, Biblical Authority) that it should break all of its ties with the federal government. With this, it dissolved its corporate status and declared that the government did not have the right to collect any taxes from church employees, for that was a violation of Baptist Principle because the church was not an arm of the government.

As a consequence of the principles of Soul Freedom and Biblical Authority, the church refused to withhold any and all taxes, which included withholding taxes as well as Social Security and Medicare taxes.

A federal prosecutor went after the church and Dixon for his refusal to pay withholding and federal income taxes, and also went after the church's bank for its laxity in these matters. Judgments were won against the church, and a twenty-acre parcel of land north of the city was seized and sold to satisfy the liens. Dixon was also found guilty of tax evasion, and the government searched for ways to satisfy the judgment against him. Despite all of these actions, only a portion of the more than five million dollar judgment was recouped.

There were years of wrangling, but in the end, to the great delight of the local television stations, federal marshals came and seized the property and sold it. Last I knew, the former church building was being used for something else. It had been sold, and the church was meeting in a public auditorium.[10]

In the end, the government got its way. The church won on the principle side, but it lost on the practical side, and in the process lost everything it owned in terms of physical facilities. Members certainly would have argued that they had a moral victory, and that the church did in fact remain intact, even minus their building.

Discussion Questions for Scenario 6

1. What are your initial thoughts as you read this scenario?
2. Do you think the church was foolish or principled in taking on the federal government?
3. Whether or not you agree with them, can you articulate the Baptist Principles involved? Why do you pick those particular Baptist Principles? How do you see them being acted out? What are the pros and cons?
4. Explain this scenario and the church's actions in terms of civil disobedience.
5. Did the government have the right to seize the church's property?
6. Even if it did have the right, should it have gone ahead with the action?
7. Do you think that justice was served in forcing the church out, by selling the building, and by stripping the church of its assets? In other words, should the church have paid such a price?
8. Should Dixon have been jailed for his refusal to "pay unto Caesar what is Caesar's" or had his assets taken away?
9. Is principle—even Baptist principle—worth losing everything?

Commentary on Scenario 6

It is a fair question to ask—what are our principles worth? It is probably fortunate that none of us has ever been asked to come to a real-

---

[10] The factual information in this paragraph and the several paragraphs prior to it was found in a Google Search, which turned up an article "Indianapolis Baptist Temple" in Wikipedia. http://en.wikipedia.org/wiki/Indianapolis_Baptist_Temple.

life decision on this; remember in the early Church how, when faced with a difficult choice, many offered libations to Caesar rather than face the lions in the Coliseum. The right of Caesar versus the freedom of conscience seems to offer the possibility of eternal discussion, choice, and conflict.

Hans Bret, an early Anabaptist, was burned at the stake in 1577 because of his Anabaptist views. Displayed in Amsterdam today is a tongue screw that was applied to his tongue as they brought him to the stake. The authorities were so much afraid that Bret would preach even in the face of his death, and they applied the screw to keep him silent. His friends later removed the tongue screw from the ashes, and it has endured—a reminder of a heroic faith that counted no cost in articulating and defending it.

There is also the story of Felix Manz who was drowned for his Anabaptist views in Zurich in 1527. Drowning was considered an apt form of execution, a cruel parody for those who insisted on Believer's Baptism. "As Manz marched to his execution, he proclaimed to all within hearing that believer's baptism was the true Christian baptism."[11]

I would make the point that, in many ways, both blatant and subtle, principled people do pay a price for standing firm in their unwavering beliefs, which they will hold in the face of opposition.

Some would argue that the cost to Baptist Temple was not martyrdom, that its cause was not justifiable. Others would argue that it was martyrdom, and surely a justifiable cause. This, of course, brings us back to the tension and the differences of interpretation on what it means to be Baptist. These are Soul Freedom and Biblical Authority issues, as well as Separation of Church and State.

Who is right? Well, isn't that a matter of interpretation? We have the right and the responsibility to disagree, but also to continue talking to each other about it, and praying with each other, and, in the end, as we will say again and again, this *is* the Baptist way.

Separation of Church and State Scenario 7

---

[11] Carol Crawford Holcom, "Where did Baptists get their name," *Baptists Today* (December 2009): 8.

Many of the individual states now have groups actively lobbying for constitutional amendments barring either abortion or homosexuality—two of our time's "hot-button" topics. Your church is large enough to have sub-groups on each side of the issue. One group wants to join in the effort for legislation because of the morality and biblical principle involved, while the other group sees such legislation as a church/state, establishment of religion issue, and therefore wants to oppose it.

Discussion Questions for Scenario 7

1. What is your initial thinking as you read this?
2. Do you decide that it is time for a series of sermons on forgiveness and reconciliation?
3. Can you articulate what the first group, the "let's legislate" group, thinks and believes?
4. Can you articulate what the second group, the establishment clause, "let's oppose" group, thinks and believes?
5. Do you consider it a healthy miracle that both groups exist in your church without doing bodily harm to each other? Is it possible for groups this divergent to coexist? What do I mean when I say, "This is the way it should be. This is the Baptist way"?
6. Someone suggests that, "freedom and responsibility are awesome gifts!" What do you think they are saying?

Separation of Church and State Scenario 8

Sitting down for supper after a long day, you and your spouse are catching up on the events of the day. Asked if anything interesting happened at the office, you speak of the Bible study group that is meeting one morning a week at the church. It is primarily geared for at-home parents of young children, and is an outreach ministry of your church, an attempt to fill a need, but to also let them see and experience the many ministries the church provides to families and to the community. At the end of the morning, the Bible study leader dropped by your office to ask if you had a moment to chat. The leader spoke of a concern that had been a topic of discussion within the group, and you were especially interested when "prayer" was mentioned as that topic.

The leader said that sometimes a topic could "get away from itself" and go in divergent directions. In this session, the topic went in the direction of teaching children prayer; this meant building a good solid base for them and their being comfortable in praying themselves. This idea then moved on to the suggestion from one of the parents, the wish in fact, that her children could include prayer in their life at the local public school, where many of the children from the church attended. Someone had mentioned that perhaps the group could take this on as a cause, bringing the matter to school officials and to the school board if necessary. Because they know you as a serious minister with excellent pastoral skills, it had been suggested that perhaps you could be the spokesperson for the group with the educational community.

Discussion Questions for Scenario 8

1. What are your initial thoughts as you read this scenario?
2. Does your spouse laugh out loud or just quietly?
3. Does your spouse comment that they are assuming that the group wants the introduction of Christian prayers?
4. Is it a good thing to teach children to pray?
5. If your answer is "yes," why wouldn't it be a good thing to teach them to pray in school? After all, school is about education.
6. What does this request have to do with the Establishment Clause of the Constitution?
7. Why is being against prayer in public schools like being against motherhood and apple pie? Or maybe it just feels that way?
8. Is prayer in public school the same thing as evangelism? At least in the eyes of some? What do you think this means?
9. From the Baptist point of view, what is the meaning of living in a pluralistic society?
10. Suppose the topic of discussion had been a request for prayer in the public school by: —A group from the Jewish synagogue? —A group from the local mosque? —A group from the local Scientology chapter? —A group from the Church of Jesus Christ Latter Day Saints?
11. Does any one in the group think that the allowance of Christian prayer should be given prominence? What basis do they have for saying that?

12. Would there be different opinions on that?
13. Should the kinds of prayers being taught be dictated by the majority?

Separation of Church and State Scenario 9

You are a young African-American minister from the South and newly serving a church there. One day your telephone rings, and a ministerial friend invites you to a meeting to strategize around some emerging community issues. The immediate focus is on the recent arrest of an African-American woman who refused to move to the rear of the bus, as law required her to do when requested by the bus driver. She had been asked to give up her seat and move, and she had been arrested when she refused and remained seated. The situation is tense, and everyone knows that this is the surface of a deep, racial divide in the culture and the mentality of the community. Going to the meeting your ministerial friends are quietly saying "When?" "If not now, when?" "We have waited too long. The time is now!" After passionate discussion, it is agreed that the African-American community will boycott the city bus system. Then someone turns, looks you in the eye and asks, "Will you lead this boycott?"

Discussion Questions for Scenario 9

1. What would your first reaction be if you were the minister in this scenario?
   —Why didn't I stay home?
   —Why didn't Rosa just move?
   —What will Coretta think?
   —What will this do to my children?
   —It's asking too much.
   —If not now, when? If not me, who?
2. Would you have, knowing the circumstances and the tension, stepped up? Why, or why not?
3. Is this civil disobedience?
4. Is civil disobedience justified in this instance?
5. What kind of price was paid?
   —By those ministers?
   —By that community?

—By the greater community of state and nation?
—By the church?

6. Can you think of other issues that call for: "If not now, when?"

Concluding Thoughts

As we come to the end of this volume, I hope that working through its chapters and concepts has not been easy for you. In fact I hope that it has been hard work – very hard work, for that will mean that you got the most out of it.

Interpreting the Bible—living out our faith—surviving in community with each other—setting priorities for the use of our resources of time, talent and treasure—can bring enormous challenges to us. There are pitfalls and detours at every turn and we must be always wary that we keep our eye on the vision of whom and what God has called us to be individually and collectively as God's Church.

It is east to be distracted—become argumentative—find a view too narrow (or perhaps too wide)—lose our passion—grow scales over our eyes or calluses over our compassion – nothing about living and thinking is easy if we want to always be everything we believe God wants us to be.

It is my strongest conviction that in our Baptist Principles there is a way through the tangles and the tensions that life brings to us every day. It is a process of discovery and discernment. It means discipline—absolute trust in God—a commitment to civility with other members of God's Body—a passion for justice in emulation of the prophets—a gift for preaching much like that of the disciples—a compassion like unto Stephen's as modeled by those "deacons" who picked up the responsibilities in the Book of Acts of caring for those in need.

We have stated often on these pages that each of the Baptist Principles is ripe with tension, with strong differing or competing feelings around a multitude of possible differences. Yet in love and with a commitment to God's work and purposes, there are tools in these Baptist Principles to move us forward and bring us together for the work with which God has entrusted us.

It is my hope and prayer that these pages have made you think and process a lot of old and new ideas, and that we all emerge with a stronger commitment to the God who revealed God's Self to us in Jesus Christ, who empowered us with God's Holy Spirit – for the task that is at hand.

To God be the Glory! Amen